Special Acknowledgment
to
Bonnie Darves
for her talent
and artful way
with this manuscript.

Acknowledgments

With every book, there is a family of loving and devoted souls who make up the cheering section. I extend my heartfelt thanks to the following:

Ruth Alben
Marjorie Powell Allen
Lilia Arguello
Miriam Bass
Pam Bernstein
Helaine Blum
Grey Boone
Jackie & Bert Briskin
Ann & Sonny Brown
David Burns
Elizabeth Cady
Paddy Calistro
Denise Cavenaugh
David Channell
Esther Channell
Susie Channell
Marilyn Cockett
Joy Colton
Susan DeNoewer
Fred Dobbs
Mary Donaghue
William E. Donoghue
Bill Doty
Jim Fawcett
Dix Fetz
Valerie Franklin
Jerry Franks
Barbara Friedman
Trish & David Glover
Dr. Robert Goodman
Elaine Taylor Gordon
Gigi & George Graveline
Peter Greenberg
Nesta & John Greth
Scott Greth
Patrice Gunn
Jo Hartley
Gail Hays
Dan Hillman
Sheri Hirst

Susan Kasen
Dee Klug
Kendall Klug
George Labovitz
Hermien Lee
Bob and Pat Lindh
Duncan McMillian
Patrick McNee
Pat & John Martin
Connie Martinson
Jeff Mason
Alex Mass
Tom Mintz
Lisa & Richard Moreno
Claudine & John Nachtrieb
Rose & Clinton Nelson
Bill Newbern
Jim Newman
Tim Nordin
Gina & Nick Osti
Robert Page
Sheila Peters
Marilyn & Kent Pelz
Howard Portugais
Soozie Reynolds
Blanche Ross
Cary Ross
Joel Rubinstein
Tom Shell
Marian Schuster
Peter Stanton
Marv & Dick Swan
Dawna Turner
Derrik Van Nimegen
Susan Lee Wax
Chris Williston
Melissa & Michael Woodruff
Patsy & Ray Woodruff
Donna & Jeff Wyant
Therese Young

For Fred Channell

The true joy of my life

Table of Contents

1

Women and the Money Mystique

I had noticed her in the audience while I was still speaking: a slender, beautifully groomed woman in her mid-thirties. She looked remarkably like Jane Pauley: the warmth, the vitality, the steady, eager gaze. I've forgotten her name, but I'll never forget what she said to me.

A break followed my part of the financial seminar. That was when she came up and introduced herself. "I just want to shake your hand," she said, "because your message is so important." I was pleased, and a little flattered, until she continued:

"My marriage has just broken up after fifteen years. My two girls are nine and seven, and I don't even know where the money is, what we're worth or anything else."

In that simple admission she threw into high relief everything I'd been trying to say that evening. She wasn't seeking answers to the complex questions of the economy or investments. This was something far more fundamental — and frightening. There she stood, Ms. America: successful, bright and self-assured. But in terms of money — its power, its pitfalls, its boundless potential for joy and self-fulfillment — she was crippled. She seemed to have two personalities. In her role as a corporate personnel manager for a large computer firm, her competence was undisputed. Yet, when it came to managing her personal finances, her involvement with money encompassed little more than buying the week's groceries and doling out the children's allowance.

"I simply assumed it was his *role* to take care of everything," she went on. "Checking accounts, savings, stocks and things like that. We had our problems, and somehow money was always in the middle of it. I see now that maybe my attitude about money was the last straw. Now, I know it's up to me to put my own house in order."

Listening to her, I remembered something I'd read in Lyn Caine's deeply moving, candid bestseller, *Widow*.

"Money matters," she said shortly after her husband's death. "It really does. It's right up there with love and security and identity."

Her husband, a bankruptcy attorney, had left their financial affairs "in a terrible mess." Ms. Caine was suddenly confronted with the problem of supporting herself and their two children. She and her husband had never discussed finances.

> It was just one of those unliberated things, I suppose, going back to the idea that little girls aren't good at math, a self-fulfilling prophecy that encourages financial incompetence. Why should any woman face deprivation and financial terror because her husband dies? Women must . . . stop playing child/wife. That role hasn't been valid for a long time.

Another victim of the Great American Shell Game was Doris Day. Despite a fabulously successful career, she found her financial affairs in a shambles after the death of her husband and business manager, Martin Melcher. Like so many other women, Ms. Day had entrusted the handling of her money to her husband. Melcher, in turn, gave over the management of their joint finances—and control of the millions his wife had earned—to his lawyer and business manager, Jerome Rosenthal.

"I was so busy working at the time, I really didn't know what was going on," Ms. Day explained. "I couldn't be at the office and the studio, too." Her suit against Rosenthal for fraud and malpractice resulted in an award of $26 million to Ms. Day. Rosenthal appealed the judgment in the California Supreme Court, where the award was affirmed. He later appealed the judgment in the United States Supreme Court, where, in March 1986, he was denied a hearing. Her case again affords dramatic evidence that you put your economic future in the hands of others at your peril. Money must become your second vocation, as Ms. Day has realized.

Unhappily, stories like these abound—and not just among widows and divorcees. Single and married women also discover too often that "nothing stings more deeply than the loss of money." The irrevocable power of money to change one's life makes itself felt most when a woman is divorced or widowed, when she receives or is deprived of money. Then it becomes personal, a direct and consuming influence. But all women feel the impact of money each moment of their lives, whether they realize it or not.

Why write a money book for women? One might rightfully assume that a distinction between the sexes is no longer necessary, but let's face reality: While we are over a decade into the women's movement, our battle for financial equality has barely been joined, much less won. *In spite of the fact that women comprise 53 percent of the population and well over half of the work force, fewer than four percent of the women in this country make over $25,000 a year.* While our power in the consumer market has long been accepted, that's a small serving indeed from the financial feast—and the unique opportunities that surround us today.

Women own 75 percent of America's stocks and bonds and 65 percent of its savings accounts. But these statistics are misleading, for two reasons: First, we live longer than men, which pushes the figures out of proportion. Second, we may own most of the nation's wealth, but don't control it. It may be held in our names — in pension funds, trust funds, insurance policies, but most of that wealth is controlled or handled by other people. *Control* is where the real action is. And the fun.

What has kept us from the joy of making rather than just spending or handling money? From the satisfaction that genuine financial responsibility ultimately brings?

One of the primary culprits is our educational system. Often the heart of the issue goes right back to those textbooks in which women are rarely shown in problem solving roles. The tendency, still with us in many school systems, is to actively discourage girls from taking an interest in mathematics, economics and finance. The end result is the often heard statement, "but I'm not any good at numbers."

But this is only half the picture. Consider today's intelligent woman, gazing apprehensively at the money-hydra with its thousand heads. It's easy enough to put the blame on her education, but that isn't the whole story. The problem runs deeper. Between woman's appointed societal role and her achievement of financial success lies a barrier so effective that it has kept us passively accepting the role of money moron for centuries: the money mystique, based on the myth that financial expertise is distinctly unfeminine. The legend goes something like this: Money is a man's game in that man's world out there, and women needn't worry their pretty little heads about it. "O frailty, thy name is woman," and all that jazz. Forget it. Women themselves have always known that they have good sense, and it is now apparent that, despite the money mystique, many women have managed to break out of this medieval financial typecasting. We *are* worrying our heads about money — some of us with spectacular results, as these pages will show. And our success has exploded the myth of the money mystique.

The idea that the female brain is somehow too feeble to grasp the intricacies of the business world dies at the hands of women like a group of nine college freshmen who, in the early 1970s, handled a $50,000 fund bequeathed to Scripps College with the stipulation that it be managed solely by women students. At the outset, none of the women had any experience in the financial area.

For three months the nine of them studied the stock market, talked with brokers, pored over *The Wall Street Journal* and other publications. They then entered the stock market—when it was in a decline. In six months they increased the fund's worth by ten percent—a far better track record than many professional money managers were achieving just then.

The making of money simply is not a sex-linked skill. Women can and are turning it all around. Recent statistics show that 25 percent of American businesses are now owned by women. We are discovering for ourselves the challenge—and the joy—of money.

Slowly but surely women are making inroads into the higher echelons of the business world. They're finding that the age-old combination of hard work, creativity and aggressive marketing can turn ideas into money-making realities. Here are just a few:

- Mary Farrar, formerly a Kansas City housewife, is now president of Hallmark Construction, a $6 million company. With knowledge gained from a part-time bookkeeping job with a steel construction firm, help from friends and supportive creditors, Mary turned her $500 down payment for used tools and ladders into a $2 million business in just two years. Six years later, she now owns two construction companies and prospects for the future are very bright.

- Lane Nemeth started Discovery Toys because she couldn't find an educational toy for a friend's one-year-old son. She couldn't drum up much interest for her idea—selling quality educational toys through home demonstrations—but her experience as director of a day-care center and results of her research convinced her that the market was out there. From her humble beginnings in the garage of her Martinez, California home with $25,000 borrowed from friends and relatives, Lane's company posted an astounding $11 million in sales in little more than two years.

"Honey, I've been rich and I've been poor," Pearl Bailey used to say. "And rich is better."

Nobody ever put it better. The joy of money can be as sweet as the joy of life, for it can bring you life's most abundant gifts, and the leisure to enjoy them. Money is time. Wisely governed, it opens a thousand doors to enrich our lives and to enable us, in turn, to enrich the world around us. Money is more than security, it is your passport to independence, to power, to control of your own future.

Money-making is also an art. Creativity, a concept not often associated with the making or managing of money, should be. On the other hand, a term like "money-grubbing" has negative connotations and shouldn't be associated with money-making. It imparts the notion that money is "vulgar" and that nice people—particularly women—shouldn't concern themselves with it. (We all know that even nice people make money!) Happily, as you will see, women are bringing their particular creative skills as never before to every aspect of the financial scene.

Making real money depends upon your ability to become financially self-assertive. Until your creative energy is freely directed toward productive financial channels, you won't become independent. Saving small amounts of money or living on a budget simply won't do the trick. When you restrict your financial horizons to careful consumerism, you are limiting a financial potential that could be boundless. The intelligent investor, woman or man, learns that risks, thoughtfully taken, can become constructive gains. Think big—but be sure you think!

You may be intelligent, you may have uncommon ability to

make others see things your way, you may have charm and self-assurance. But none of these qualities will significantly change your financial prospects until you summon the will and knowledge to put it all together. To make money work creatively for you, you must first become creative in your own thinking about money. At the outset, it will take a lot of hard work, ruthless self-examination and disciplined observation of the ground rules. It then takes courage and imagination to make your first flight and to maintain altitude. Be resilient and flexible; be open to new ideas. You will take pride in having developed your competence in money matters, and you will find that the rewards accompanying that pride can be spectacular.

Once you've set your course for financial liberation, once you've assessed where your best talents lie and how much you can realistically hope to achieve—most of all, once you have built the confidence to conquer your fear of the money world—you will be free to respond to its exciting challenges. Once you're able to cope with flair and distinction in big and small ways, you will find the money game the best in town. Here we're playing for keeps. And the stakes are your future.

My own financial education was anything but traditional. While many people are introduced to the money world through their own personal finances or college economics courses, I slipped in through the side door of corporate finance. At the time, I actually knew more about corporate underwritings and the stock market than how to keep my checkbook straight.

At nineteen, I started working for a small aerospace manufacturing company headed by Peter Stanton, a successful entrepreneur. The economy at the time was in a definite upswing, and much of the talk around me was geared to when the Dow Jones Industrial Average would break 1000. (Broadway even had a hit entitled *How Now, Dow Jones*). It was a fascinating introduction to the business world—and I'd have to have been deaf, dumb and blind not to have caught the electricity in the financial air in those days.

I learned a lot simply by osmosis; looking and listening, and reading *The Wall Street Journal.* Since the company I'd joined was small, I was able to sit in on many of the financial meetings and watch the decision-making process at work. At the time, I hadn't yet made the connection between the sense of excitement I felt and my own participation in the exercise of power. Now I realize how large a part that very sensation played in attracting me to the business world.

After a time the glow wore off, to be replaced by a more serious attitude. I had decided to become a businesswoman; and though I knew I'd stumbled into the world of business and finance by a lucky accident, I was determined to stay there by design. And my timing was perfect.

During this period the aerospace company was sold, and I joined forces with Peter Stanton and an electronics engineer in a new venture. It was called Infonics, Inc., and I took charge of its sales and marketing program. In three years Infonics, a manufacturer of audio equipment, grew from a fledgling three-person company into a multi-million-dollar corporation. A Los Angeles newspaper reported in a four-column spread that "Paula Nelson has increased the company's sales by 400 percent in two-and-a-half years. She does business with 100 dealers in the United States and has now set up 24 distributors abroad."

It was obviously an exciting time for me—in fact, it seemed I could do no wrong. The crowning moment came in 1969, when Infonics had a public stock issue, and the stock climbed from $5 a share to more than $26.

For many of us, money becomes real all at once, without any advance warning. It did for me, when I realized the value of the stock option I held, and figured out that it represented a potential ticket to financial independence. For another women, that reality may come after receiving an inheritance or a divorce settlement. However it comes, it's the first time she sees money as "my" money.

But money that isn't supported by adequate knowledge and planning can vanish almost as suddenly as it appeared. It's one thing to carve out a corporate niche for yourself, earn a handsome salary and capitalize on a stock option, and quite another to assume the responsibility of seizing the financial opportunity that your income and position have made possible.

Like many single women, I found I was floating in a kind of economic holding pattern, waiting for someone to come along and take charge of that part of my life. It was *A Doll's House* all over again. I was a corporate executive, and a good one, but in terms of my personal finances I was acting like a 19th century hausfrau. Financial responsibility, finally, is every individual's problem and opportunity. If I evaded either, I would have to accept whatever I was handed. And that I didn't want.

It was time to shift gears. I decided that money must, in a very real sense, become my "second vocation"—that is, if I was to keep any of my nest egg. The big question was: Where do I begin? My first thought—to turn the entire kit and kaboodle over to a financial advisor—quickly fizzled when I learned that the best money managers have little interest in accounts under $1,000,000. I then talked to friends and associates, who presented dozens of enthusiastic schemes, from olive groves to oil wells. Still others insisted that the stock market was the only place to make any *real* money. I came away horrified by my own ignorance and that of most of my friends. I had gained a mishmash of contradictory information, half-baked plans, and precious few of the hard facts I needed to build a secure financial foundation. That was when I decided to sit down with my yellow pad and pencil, and use the same logic that I had always used in business.

And it worked.

The first step was assembling a financial photograph in order to find out exactly what I was worth. It was refreshing to find that I had much more to work with than I had realized.

Next, I set down my immediate financial goals and then I brainstormed, letting my imagination roam free, while tempering it with a sense of hard reality, in order to develop a five-year plan. Yes, five whole years ahead.

The third step was determining what financial tools I needed to achieve my five-year goal. I had learned through experience that certain top professionals — brokers, lawyers, bankers, or accountants — are indispensible in the business world. I needed to know how to select these professionals, how to develop the art of asking the right questions in order to determine the profit potential of a particular investment and whether it was right for me.

My final step was to figure out which options were open and available to me, in harmony with my interests and skills — and within my reach. I've found that many people wander around wearing financial blinders, looking at only one small corner of the money world. Early on, I thought the stock market was the only royal road to riches. In fact, the options for making money and investing it are virtually limitless — and therein lies the opportunity and the problem.

The point is a crucial one: If you are to achieve success in the financial world, you must discover your true interests and talents. In my third book, *Paula Nelson's Guide to Getting Rich*, I define this concept as your "Economic Orbit of Opportunity." Each of us has one, and it comprises all the factors that make our environment, experiences and economic assets unique from everyone else's. The Economic Orbit is the city you live in, the publications you read, the people you know, the hobbies you enjoy. It includes your paycheck, credit rating, retirement package, education, career and special areas of expertise. Your Economic Orbit gives you valuable insights into money-making opportunities you probably don't even know you have. Once you've determined yours, dig in, dig deep and specialize. What excites you? Is it the stock market? Real estate? Art or antiques? Commodities, gold, or cotton futures? Or do you long to launch your own company, however small?

Everyone comes to the question of skills and interests with a different supply of emotional and financial resources and the decision is consequently a very personal one. It is vital, nonetheless. An astute choice—for you—can be rewarding indeed. Only after I had defined my own "orbit" could I begin the creative process of effective money-making and managing.

The era of the knowledgeable, competent woman in business is clearly fully entrenched. The big breakthroughs have been made. It may be unusual (mighty unusual!) to earn a staggering seven-figure salary like Barbara Walters, but the $30,000 to $50,000 a year range is a readily attainable goal. Today women of any age need no longer wait for a financial Prince Charming. Women today have proved we can pull our financial weight, and we intend to keep right on doing so with a new spirit of confidence. We've found that the biggest obstacle toward realizing that "second vocation" is the fear of failure—or success. We've even found out how much fun it can be. More and more we are looking to ourselves, to our newly aroused consciousness of the role that money can and should play in our lives. We also know it is unfair—yes, unfair—for men to carry alone the burden of total financial responsibility.

I have experienced my own "financial awareness evolution," and I know the rewards that come with it. I also know that it doesn't happen overnight and cannot happen in a vacuum. This book will not offer effortless shortcuts to boundless riches, or guarantee that you will become a millionaire in two years. I do believe that the shortest route to your financial freedom lies in knowing yourself, knowing what you need to do to achieve your goals and realizing that those goals are attainable. Once you accept your own financial responsibility and start achieving your own definable economic goals, making money will provide a new dimension to your life.

We all like skiing at St. Moritz or swimming off Sardinia—

but those momentary pleasures simply don't compare to the deeper excitement that comes from having your own ability create for you a *lasting* freedom. If you're married, you and your husband can experience the pleasure of working toward the fulfillment of common goals. Money is too important to be the source of bickering. It's one of the realities of life. Face it and enjoy it.

When I asked a young California busineswoman how she would rate the importance of money on a scale of one to ten, her reply was simple and direct: "Eleven."

This is not to suggest that you must become obsessed by money. Any obsession is boring, and a subject as fascinating as money should never become a bore. Money is indeed a good servant and a bad master. What I'm speaking for is freedom — the freedom money can bring, the opportunity to expand your horizons, the chance to do what you really want to do with your life.

Creatively pursued, money can work for you, grow for you, and help you to discover the unique satisfaction of shaping and controlling your own future. As I hope you will discover, that's the real joy of money.

2
Goals: You CAN Get There From Here

We had scheduled the interview for the hour following my seminar at the Ambassador Hotel in Los Angeles. Shirley Chilton has been called dynamic, personable and talented. A firm believer in goals, Shirley rose from a position as switchboard operator to become Chairman of the Board of Daniel Reeves and Company, a member of the New York Stock Exchange headquartered in Los Angeles.

My first question was: "What do you consider the key element in your business success?"

"I'm a goal-setter," she said, "and I've made goals for myself ever since childhood. When I was nine, my goal was to become the best student I possibly could. I ended up being valedictorian of my class. Ever since, I've set short- and long-term goals, and tried to achieve each of them in a specified period of time. This is every bit as important after you've won a certain position as before. Right now, I'm planning what I'll do after I retire."

Read that last sentence again. That's the most significant thing about Shirley's grand design: She has gone far beyond the typical one-year or five-year goal—she has a life plan. Whereas most of us entertain some fantasies about spending our retirement gardening or traveling, Shirley knows exactly what she wants and has already begun preparing for it: She's going to be writing children's books that deal with economics and how our free enterprise system works.

Once you've decided to achieve your own financial freedom you must, from the start, define your financial goals. This means asking yourself some intriguing questions. What, specifically, is your own particular long-range money goal? Do you want to be rich—really rich? Do you want to own and run your own company? Or do you simply want to have enough money so that you need never worry about not having as much as you want? An economic goal can be time-oriented rather than money-oriented. Bonnie Lynch, a Los Angeles travel agent, defined her goal as being able to work only six months a year and make enough money to spend the other six months doing as she pleased.

Perhaps your long-range goal involves a combination of some or all of the above—or none of the above. Whatever it is, you'll need to decide at the outset. Then you'll be ready to get down to shorter-term goal strategy.

Goals need to be established in at least three time chunks: short-term (one year), intermediate (three years), and long-term (five years). Actually pinpointing a dollar goal is often extremely difficult, but it can be done, and it is absolutely vital. If you're an excellent planner like Shirley Chilton, you might work at developing a twenty-year or life plan. But, initially, these three phases covering five years are adequate. Most people, once they've developed goals, tend to get hooked on them for one simple reason: They work.

Here are my own suggestions for financial goal planning:

1. *Write down your goals, or type them up.* You need to pin yourself down on this: It's your visible, tangible commitment.

2. *Keep your goals high, but realistic.* Billie Jean King

worked and willed herself to become a great tennis champion —
and then used that position to become publisher of a women's
sports magazine. She didn't try to become a film star or a foreign
affairs adviser to the President. She knew where her field of
excellence lay, and she moved, very successfully, within that
framework. Your financial goals must be guided by the same
healthy practicality. Obviously, planning to buy in the near future
property worth $150,000 on an annual income of $25,000 is
anything but realistic.

3. *Always set a time frame in which to achieve a goal.* A
promotion in one year, say; or owning your own firm in three
years; or an annual salary of $200,000 in five years. This will not
only enable you to keep a watchful eye on your progress, it will
also force you to ask yourself some critical questions. Are you
being paid enough in your present job? Does your employer place
an adequate value on your talents? Above all, are you drifting in
your current job, just doing what has to be done without
developing a sense of direction?

4. *Establish mini-goals as stepping-stones to major goals, and
quantify them in terms of the time and money (if any) required to
achieve them.* Setting minimal goals in themselves — telling
yourself you'll take this if you can't have that, and then you'll be
satisified — is obviously self-defeating. Minimal goals are every
woman's great pitfall: Don't fall for them. When Helen Gurley
Brown took over the editorship of *Cosmopolitan*, her presumed
goal was to get the magazine back on the profitable side of the
ledger. Instead of aiming at a general readership, she selected one
market she knew a great deal about, the single girl, and set out to
capture it. The circulation figures, advertising and balance sheets
of Cosmo demonstrate that she was right in focusing on one
specific market — but with the larger goal always in view.

5. *Change your goals when your circumstances change.*
Remember that rules are made to be broken, when the occasion
demands. Review your progress in ninety days or six months.

Don't make rules for yourself so rigid that they can't be changed. Money is probably the most fluid commodity in the world today (as the following chapters will show), and you need to keep your program flexible, even as you keep your overall effort consistent.

6. *Take immediate action*. Don't procrastinate on this; it's the most important point of all. "Opportunity once forsaken is opportunity lost forever," as Omar Bradley, the celebrated "GIs' general," put it, and that's every bit as true in the world of business. There's a niche for you out there in real estate or electronics or corporate finance, but you'll never fill it if you sink back into the nine-to-five syndrome, or wait for manna from heaven, or go around murmuring, "this job will do until I get married." Says economist Peter Drucker: "The future will not just happen if one wishes hard enough. It requires decision—now. It imposes risk—now. It requires action—now." Set it out on a sheet of paper:

FINANCIAL GOALS

Goal	$ Cost	Date Begun	Achievement Date

The key to creating and defining your goals is the quality and depth of a personal question-and-answer session. You have to face yourself first. Then, if you are developing a family financial goal, you should work closely with your husband and your older children. Raise their financial consciousness, for they ought to be an integral part of the effort and achievement. I'm not talking about budget meetings, but horizon sessions. They can be fun— and productive.

My own family was involved in land and real estate. Some of my early memories are of sitting with my parents across the desk from Donna Swink, head of the escrow department at the Santa Monica Bank. I remember listening to the discussions, watching everyone go through and sign the papers, seeing the checks exchanged. Occasionally I went along with my parents to talk to real estate people. I saw houses bought and sold, and once when I was nine and my parents were out, I showed a house to some interested buyers. I simply mimicked all the things I'd heard my mother say, even discussing the terms of payment!

I've always felt that I was lucky to have this kind of early exposure. It's one of the factors that freed me of much of the fear of the financial world that has gripped so many women.

Back to goals: It's important to open up your mind and allow yourself creative dreaming in the course of developing your goals. What do I want to be, where do I want to be? How much do I want to be worth? However, it's equally important for that creative dreaming to evolve into a concrete, reasonable, step-by-step plan. If the dream won't conform, drop that one and try another.

Here are sixteen questions that will help you start the thinking process:

1. Are you currently engaged in a career?
2. Are you considering changing careers or upgrading?
3. Are you thinking of returning to college for a degree?
4. Are you about to have a change in personal status: About to be married? About to be divorced?
5. Are you permanently single (by choice)?
6. Do you already have children?
7. Are you likely to have a child in the next year or two?
8. Are you a single head of your household?
9. What are your sources of income? Salary? Dual income? Alimony? Investments? Others?
10. Are you now or are you about to become responsible for another person, such as a parent or spouse (returning to school or disabled)?
11. Are you nearing retirement age? How far ahead can you plan?
12. Do you have some major purchase (house, car, etc.)

13. planned for the next year or two?
13. Do you plan to relocate in this country?
14. Do you want to live abroad?
15. How much time do you have available now for financial planning and education?
16. Do you have any viable, money-making ideas? If so, list them.

There are, of course, many questions that could be added to the list, but these will at least get you started and give you a basis from which to think and act. Just knowing the answers to these questions isn't enough, though. You must allow for—and plan for—changes in your life, even if they appear obvious now. They will have a significant and lasting effect on your financial life and profile. One of the primary purposes of goal-setting is to clarify your thinking, to force yourself to think through the situation in actuality, and then to project into the future and define how and with what tools your goal can be accomplished.

One interesting tool, the "blank check" technique, may be useful to you. It is often used by employers of highly motivated salespeople to help them stretch their thinking about how much they want to earn. Simply take a blank check, make it out to yourself, and fill in the amount you want to earn this year, or what you want to be worth in ten years.

This isn't as silly as it sounds. Writing out the check serves two purposes: It makes you think through precisely how much money you really want to have. Also, writing it down formally in this way constitutes a kind of mental commitment to the idea. It's an excellent personal motivator—if you don't make the check out for too little.

Next, try to relate your target to your own special skills or interests. At a recent financial mini-seminar, I asked six women to write down their long-range goals. From the six, we selected Carla James's objectives to be reviewed by the group. Carla, the mother of three children, is nearing forty. She had two goals. The first was to put her three children through college; the second was to retire to a farm in her native Ohio.

After some discussion and figuring we determined that she would need roughly $200,000 over the next ten years. This figure is considerably less frightening when you break it down to $20,000 per year. Carla now had her financial goal. In other words, she had translated her goal into dollars. The next question was how to build that $200,000—which forces us all to get creative. We asked her question after question to get a profile of her capabilities and interests. She was working in the escrow department of a bank; before that she had been involved in real estate. Her response was quick. "Why don't I go into real estate, get my license? It seems so simple. Why didn't I see it before this?"

In fact, she did two things. She took immediate action; she signed up for a real estate license course that same day, and she also talked with several friends who were interested in finding the best possible real estate property investment in the area. She would do the research and legwork involved, she told them, in exchange for a percentage of the property. It took her six weekends, combing the real estate sections of the Sunday newspapers and marching through duplexes all over San Francisco, before she was ready to present two possible properties to her new partners. They selected one, and an attorney drew up a contract. Carla was given ten percent of the property; in exchange for twelve days' intensive work she was a $7000 partner in a real estate investment.

It all came about because she established an attainable financial goal, related it to her capabilities and enthusiasm, took immediate action, and kept her sights right on the target. As a happy postscript, she is now a successful real estate broker in San Francisco—and that initial investment sold several years ago for well over $150,000, more than doubling her initial $7,000 to $15,000.

The final link to your goal planning, then, is a relentless probe of your areas of interest and competence. The questions that follow are crucial, for they will help you establish your financial direction:

1. What are your interests and hobbies?
2. Do you have a flair for real estate, coins, furniture, stamps, art, flowers, cars, the stock market?
3. Are you creative? Can you write, paint, sculpt, build, whatever?
4. What areas of specialized knowledge do you have, however irrelevant they may seem now?

If you don't seem to have any particular interest or strong suits, do some vocational shopping. Go to your local college and audit classes that cover various areas of investment, or join finance seminars. If one subject doesn't spark you, go on to the next. Your niche is there, but you must find it. And if this looks like a lot of legwork, it is. "No pain, no gain," as the old saying goes.

Above all, be venturesome. Rigidity is death to a creative money career approach. And don't be afraid to follow your "gut feeling." If the field in question is one you know something about, you'll find your instincts are generally reliable. Often enough the most modest opening can become your particular highway to financial self-realization.

In my own case, I'd been plodding along for a year as a secretary-researcher with Aerospace Components Corporation. When I learned that my boss, contracts administrator for Aerospace, was leaving the company in a cutback, I managed to convince the brass that I had equipped myself to take over his job. What actually happened here was that management decided to save another expensive salary and give me the title and responsibility, but that was all right with me. I knew that to lift myself out of the ranks of the typewriter brigade, I had to first gain administrative experience and then maneuver myself into a position where my competence would be highly visible.

About the same time I took over as contracts administrator, Stanton acquired another small company (later to be called Infonics). It was so small, in fact, that it was operated in a 14-by-16-foot room, the same building with Aerospace, which allowed me to become involved in all its operations. I quickly became totally fascinated with the product line — tape duplicators — and I found myself being invited to sit in on meetings practically from day one.

My own personal moment of truth came about a year later when Peter Stanton told me he had decided to sell Aerospace and devote all his time to the building of the new venture, Infonics, Inc. Would I be interested in coming along as sales manager and a corporate officer? I hesitated, but not for long. I had a natural flair for selling, and I knew it. I'd found that out when I successfully handled the Infonics booth at a Los Angeles convention several months before. I knew the product inside and out, and I believed in it. I had developed complete confidence in Stanton's business acumen and drive. And I knew that I could best reach my own goals through participation in a fledgling company in a field with high growth potential.

And we brought it off. Two years later, while attending a trade fair, Peter Stanton and I were sipping brandy one night at the Principe e Savoia in Milan with our German distributor when we received a transatlantic call from George Otis, one of our associates. He announced that the Infonics stock had zoomed from $5 to $26 a share, or 200 times earnings; at that moment, one of us had become a millionaire and the other very comfortable . . . at least on paper. Unfortunately I wasn't the millionaire, but I was hardly complaining. (What a feeling of celebration a moment like that brings; a sense of triumph that is unrivaled!)

That's how, in my early twenties, I skipped the long, weary climb through the executive echelons and vaulted at a bound into the entrepreneurial ranks. I took a chance on a small outfit that presented a marvelous opportunity—as well as a few big ifs. True, we could haven fallen on our faces, in which case I would have had to go back to square one. But my point here is that if you want to break out of the confines of the Friday paycheck treadmill, you need to recognize your opportunity when it arises, and then have the courage to seize that chance and make the most of it. *Carpe diem.* Gather ye rosebuds. Oh, yes. Before it's too late.

The other side of that coin is illustrated by a woman who, thanks to her exceptional capabilities in organizing and running the internal affairs of my department, freed me to function in those areas for which I was best suited. On at least six separate occasions I brought up the possibility of her becoming a manager herself, but she always turned it down. And my offers were not the only ones she had. To this day I believe she could have been enormously successful in many areas of management, but she either would not or could not make that frightening leap to freedom.

Perhaps, too, she was feeling not fear or failure, but that distinctly feminine malediction, fear of success. Sounds crazy, doesn't it? But listen to Matina Horner, President of Radcliffe College, who gave standard TAT achievement motivation tests to a sample group of 90 female and 88 male students at the University of Michigan. She found that the brightest girls, odd as it may seem, were caught in a double bind that made them wary of reaching their greatest potential.

In testing and other achievement-oriented situations, Dr. Horner found the bright girl worries not only about failure but also about success. If she fails, she is not living up to her own standards of performance; if she succeeds, she is not living up to societal expectations about the female role. Men in our society do not experience this kind of ambivalence, because they are not only permitted but actively encouraged to do well.

Obviously a young woman conscious of what Dr. Horner calls the "Psychological Barrier" to feminine success, isn't likely to set high goals for herself.

For a healthy antidote to this kind of diffidence, I enthusiastically urge you to find yourself a role model, someone who has achieved to the fullest what you're seeking, or who stands for marked excellence in your field. Imitation isn't only the sincerest form of flattery, it creates incentive. And it's not just a spur, but an ego-builder, too. You see that other women have left from humbler starting blocks than yours and have won their races. "She has done it," you can say to yourself at a particularly trying moment. "I can, too." Above all, the one cure for the fear of success syndrome is action. Trying things, taking risks. Don't allow yourself to be a stat in a Harvard study. The one option we all possess is to choose *not* to fear success, but to revel in it — and others will revel with you.

Of all the personal success stories I've known, the one that has most inspired me is that of Shirley R. Chilton, whom I've mentioned earlier. I first learned about her in a *Los Angeles Times* article, years before I made my own break for freedom. I was so impressed by her accomplishments that I wrote her and telephoned her once or twice, and although I didn't meet her until long after the Infonics venture had succeeded, she became for me the living example of what a woman can do when she is properly motivated and defines her goals — and, just as important — she disproves the tired old bromide that women involved in the financial world are "unfeminine." A vigorous, charming woman, Shirley Chilton is both a resounding business success and a devoted wife and mother.

The stepping stones of her career are lessons in themselves. Upon U.S. entry into World War II, she served on the switchboard of the Bremerton Naval Station, handling top secret traffic to the Pacific war fronts.

Mathematics had always fascinated her. "Through it I became interested in economics, and then in business and finance." Her education has been a continuing process. After special courses at

Harvard, Columbia, the University of Southern California and UCLA, she took her master's degree at Pepperdine and went on to get her doctorate.

The jobs she held on her steady ascent to the financial heights suggest that unflagging energy with which she conquered a masculine province, always guided by her belief that "women are as knowledgeable as men if they are as dedicated to the field in which they operate." She was a flight crew instructor for United Airlines, an accountant for the Packard Bell Company, secretary of a Seattle corporation; she then moved down to Los Angeles and joined Daniel Reeves and Company.

In 1972, after Reeves's death, she held various positions from security analyst and portfolio adviser at Daniel Reeves and Company to president and chief executive officer—with nine men as the other partners who chose her for the number one spot. She then went on to become Chairman of the Board.

I learned a great many things from studying Shirley Chilton's career. Here are a few of them:

1. *Don't be satisfied with a title unless either more compensation or more responsibility goes with it.* (In my own case with Aerospace, I took the title because, despite the initially unsatisfactory salary, the authority to make some management decisions, and access to more knowledge about the product, came with it.)

2. *Don't stay in a job that bores you, even if the salary is good.* Ultimately it'll prove a dead end. You need to find satisfaction (genuine excitement, ideally) in the work if you're going to make a success of it.

3. *Don't underrate yourself. (Plenty of other people will always be willing to do that job for you.)* Having achieved competence in your job, you should aim for the next rung up the company ladder, or for a position that promises fulfillment as well as opportunity. Always appraise your potential on the basis of the most rather than the least you can accomplish.

4. *Don't fritter away time.* This is a vital factor in achieving

financial self-realization. If your job doesn't pay well enough to allow you to make a start on your financial independence, look for a better one. Job-hopping is frowned on by some employers, but remember—their concern is corporate, yours is personal. Preeminently successful women haven't let mobility stand in their way. Neither should you. The possibility of a pension bestowed at the end of a long but unprofitable service to a company (and unprofitable to you) should have no allure whatsoever.

Obviously a certain venturesome quality is necessary if you're going to make the most of the steadily increasing equality of opportunity in the business world. At some point or other you will have to take risks, trust your instincts. You cannot be inhibited by unfounded fears, or by people who do not share your vision of what you can accomplish. Confidence is the name of the game. And so is creative assertiveness. Analyzing your current situation, developing goals, deriving inspiration from role models, and enlarging your vision of what you can achieve will for the indispensible base for your program of financial freedom. A note of caution here. Goals are great—and essential. They can, however, be a trap. Here's how the trap works. You read this chapter, ask yourself the important questions, and carefully write out your goals. Then you take the fruits of your efforts, file them away, and expect somehow that things will just begin to happen. *They won't!* Goals are simply a staple to take with you on your journey to achieving a dream. The key to avoiding the goal trap is instant action.

3

The Money Diet:
You Can't Be Too Rich Or Too Thin

Once you've decided to make money work for you, to use it in shaping and controlling your own destiny, you'll usually find that the first thing you need to do is straighten out your personal finances. You're probably in debt, right? Debt may be the American Way of Life, but it's not for you. You will have to get out of that hole before you can begin climbing toward your objective.

The money diet — moving yourself from the debit to the credit side of the ledger — is essential in achieving your long-range goal of financial liberation. It sounds simple: You stop spending and start saving. But, as most of us know from bitter experience, it isn't that easy. It's much the same problem, in fact, that people confront when they want to stop putting on weight and begin losing it. The tough part is reversing the process. That's why I suggest a strict dieting regimen.

You won't win your financial independence until and unless you achieve a favorable credit position. People simply aren't going to trust you with money, or give you the funds you may need to start your own business or initiate an investment plan or purchase real estate, until you've proved yourself responsible. And bing in unpurposeful debt — *personal* debt — is not responsible.

Like most women, I had virtually no training in how to handle money. When I was in grade school my classmates and I were introduced to the school banking program, into whose tin coffers we were supposed to deposit twenty-five cents a week. And that was the beginning and the end of my formal financial education.

By the time I was in my teens and working part time, I found myself in a distressing credit situation. "Neither a borrower nor a lender be?" Fine, but I wasn't reading much Shakespeare. I was six months behind, on an average, in paying my debts. Having induced my parents to co-sign the applications, I'd acquired a number of charge accounts. I'd get my paycheck one day, and by the next day it had vanished into the waiting hands of my creditors. Sound familiar? The Great American Debt System was at work. If it works for everyone else, I thought, why shouldn't it work for me?

But of course it doesn't work for everyone else either. Naturally I felt sophisticated and independent, being able to march into department stores and charge whatever caught my fancy. I simply had no sense of the reality of money. It was there, sometimes; that was all. I didn't realize how much of my income was being drained away in paying all the interest on revolving charge accounts for all the money I owed. I was on a treadmill that, for many Americans, keeps them jogging in one place for the rest of their lives. I was a financial disaster area before I was old enough to legally sign a contract.

By the time I'd turned twenty-three I was earning a handsome salary and dealing with sizable financial matters on the corporate level. I was a "success" — but on the personal level the picture was different, and depressing. All that money coming in merely meant that I could have a Mercedes instead of a Mustang, an elegant beachfront apartment, and designer clothes. It simply hadn't occurred to me that I had to manage my own affairs as wisely as a successful company manages its affairs.

The thought of putting part of my salary to work for me, of investing in something besides personal indulgence, hadn't entered my mind. The world of personal investments was a never-never land — single women just didn't go in for that sort of thing. It was part of what I call the Prince Charming Syndrome: You wait for Mr. Right to come along, sweep you off your feet and take charge of your pampered future. A Tom Selleck, say, with the business acumen of J. Paul Getty. . . .

It took me three years to come to my senses. At twenty-four I realized that liberation portended more than changing legalities; it threw open a world of unimagined possibilities. A woman could design and assume responsibility for her own future. My identity was there for the taking. I began going out and seeking advice in the financial field, attending seminars for women in similar situations, and building up a small financial library. That step ultimately changed my world — because I am now in control of it.

Before that awakening (like many of you, I imagine), I tried various means of extricating myself from the quicksands of easy credit. One deceptively painless method is the debt consolidation plan: Typically a bank or finance company asks you to bring in all of your bills and then makes a loan to you amounting to the total of all these bills plus a little extra for ready spending. With the loan you have received, you pay off all of your bills and are left only with the loan payable to the finance company. Frequently the interest charged by the finance company exceeds the interest charged by your previous creditors. Equally important, the period of time over which the loan is payable generally exceeds the average of the various bills it replaces. Since paying this stretched-out loan is relatively painless, you have a tendency to make new purchases and sink back into the morass of debt all over again.

That's what happened to me. Disregarding the warning of Bill Kuhns, a banker friend, I had my debts consolidated through a bank loan. It took me just three months to get in trouble all over again. All this time the bank was collecting twelve percent on the money it had laid out for my creditors — just another bill added to new charges.

The truth, of course, is that there isn't any easy, painless way to get out of debt. *It is going to hurt.* You have to rid yourself of the idea that you're standing under some gigantic, inexhaustible money cornucopia. You must convince yourself that it really isn't un-American to jump off the perpetual getting/spending merry-go-round.

Your first goal is to get in control of your situation by pinning down specifically what it is that you have to tackle. (Which, as a fringe benefit, is also an excellent way of beating down panic.) There are two key steps here. The first is to determine your net worth today; the second is to anticipate your expenses and income for the next twelve months. These two documents are all that is required — but they are absolute musts.

Think of your Net Worth Calculation as a financial photograph of the dollar and cents side of you. We all have a net worth, but few of us know what it is. Your net worth can be negative as well as positive: you may owe more than you own. If you *are* in trouble, the most important thing you can do is move right down the list to find out precisely how far in debt you are. Then and only then can you establish a plan of action.

Your Net Worth Calculation should be made at least once a year, unless you undergo some drastic change. Then you may have to do it more often. To calculate your net worth you will need to assemble various documents and perhaps do some research with your bank, employer, or stockbroker. The most important element is determining the current market value of your house, car, jewelry, art and other assets. Establishing current market value (what an item is worth *today*) can be done through various channels: Ads in your local newspaper, checking with your real estate broker or, for your own car, checking the famous Blue Book. What will all this tell you? How much you are worth, what you own; and it will give you a financial photograph as well as a selling tool to use with your banker when applying for a loan.

The following form is simply a suggested outline; you will undoubtedly have to make special additions or deletions. Your calculation should be done formally. And I suggest that you keep it in a permanent folder, tagged "Jane Doe, Net Worth," or "Doe Family, Net Worth"—and be sure you date it. This is, by the way, the same type of calculation a company makes at least once a year. So you are, in effect, treating yourself like a corporation.

SUGGESTED NET WORTH CALCULATION
NET WORTH STATEMENT
OF

_____

DATE

Assets	*(Fill in amount)*
Cash on hand . . . . $ _____	
Checking accounts . . . . _____	
Savings accounts . . . . _____	
Corporate profit-sharing plans—money now due you . . . . _____	
Marketable stocks (lower of cost or present market value) . . . . _____	
Money you have lent someone . . . . _____	
Life insurance (total cash surrender value) . . . . _____	
Bonds, including U.S. government . . . . _____	
Real Estate	
Home (at market value) . . . . _____	
Investment properties . . . . _____	
Syndications . . . . _____	
Automobile(s), current market value . . . . _____	
Furs, jewelry, antiques, paintings (market value) . . . . _____	
Total Assets . . . . $ _____	

Liabilities   *(Fill in amount)*

Unapid bills

    Charge accounts .... _____

    Credit card accounts .... _____

    Taxes (payable in next 12 months)........................ _____

    Insurance premiums (payable in next 12 months) .... _____

    Rent .... _____

    Installment contracts .... _____

Loans: Banks

    Savings and loans .... _____

    Insurance companies.................................... _____

    Credit unions .... _____

    Car loans .... _____

Mortgages

    House and other real property........................... _____

Total Liabilities ....$_____

Summary of Net Worth Calculation

Assets ....$_____

Liabilities ....$_____

Net worth

    (assets minus liabilities) ....$_____

Now that you've filled out your personal balance sheet, you know where you stand. Look hard at those two bottom lines. Do your liabilities exceed your assets? If so, you are in trouble, and no two ways about it.

Debt is the slavery of the free, somebody said — some poor devil who undoubtedly went through it all. Once you've committed yourself to escape from the slavery of easy credit, you're ready for the money diet of programmed spending.

First, take pencil and paper and make a list. The list, O Debtor, will be a careful breakdown — an analysis of each bill or obligation — of just how deep in debt you are. This has its sobering side, I know, but you're going to face it now, resisting the temptation to shove that accusing column of figures in a drawer. The list is vital: It's not only proof that you're meeting your predicament head-on; it's also a major component of your liquidation program.

Next, you work up an Accounts Payable Aging or Debt Aging. This has nothing to do with your getting old and turning gray (at least, not directly). It's a common business term, and it simply means determining how much you owe, and how old each of those outstanding bills is. Then list and date them according to whether they are 30, 60 or 90 days old. A typical accounts payable aging form looks like this:

DEBT AGING
(How Old)

Debt or Bill (example)	30 Days	60 Days	90 Days	Over 90
ABC Dept. Store		$160.03		
Dr. Jones	$27.00			

Next, determine what portion of your income you can spare to pay off those bills on a monthly basis. That is the amount that needs to be divided into the total of all the bills outstanding. Then decide which bill cries out to be paid first. Here's one way of looking at it: If you have a credit card account on which you're paying 19 percent interest, you may be better off getting a loan from a bank at, say, 14 percent, in order to pay it off. Yes, this is a form of debt consolidation, but when interest rates are extremely high, it may make sense to go for that loan.

Now you're ready to act. You must take command of the situation, having lost control of it by slipping into debt. Your first move is to quiet your creditors, not to avoid them or try to evade paying them—because an eventual good credit rating will be crucial to your effort to make yourself financially independent.

No matter how tough he or she has been with you in the past, your creditor is likely to be sympathetic if you offer your own, not a bank's or loan company's, debt consolidation plan. Your creditor values candor — possibly because he doesn't encounter it too often. His goal is to get paid, if not in 30 days, then eventually. If it takes you a year to pay off what you owe, he's still in better shape than if he has to dip into his bad-debt reserve.

So write your creditors, frankly outlining your situation. Tell them exactly how you propose to go about paying and the amount you will send them every week or month. The worst thing that can happen is that they'll turn your plan down — which, with the prospect of eventual payment, they rarely do. A realistic plan is sure to meet with understanding. The letter should be sent to all your creditors, including department stores — even though this move is quite likely to result in the temporary suspension of your charge privileges (which may be a blessing in disguise).

You must remember that this program will work only once. After those envelopes drop through the slot, you're committed. You cannot expect your creditors, who have agreed to your proposal, to be as amiable if you send out a second series of letters begging off. The essential point is to propose a payoff rate that won't cripple you, and then stick to the program, no matter how much it hurts.

Once you've reached an agreement with your creditors, you should take a long, hard look at your fixed expenses and eliminate all purchasing that isn't strictly necessary. And this means — you guessed it — budgeting: or what I prefer to call a money plan.

Consumer Credit Counseling — Hope for the Hopeless

If you've fallen into the Great American Debt Trap, and can't find your way out, you may be a candidate for credit counseling. Unfortunately, many women find that their ability to obtain credit is greater than their income-producing ability, and consequently fall deeper and deeper into debt.

If you can't break the pattern, get help. Most cities have non-profit credit counseling agencies that offer guidance on how to get out and stay out of debt. A counselor studies your life-style, determines how much of your income is needed for day-to-day living, and shows you how the remainder can be used to pay outstanding bills. The service is free in most states, and only a nominal fee is levied in others. To locate the agency nearest you, write to the National Foundation for Consumer Credit, Inc., 1819 H Street, N.W., Washington, D.C.

Chapter 13 and Bankruptcy — The Last Resort

Although it is part of the bankruptcy law, Chapter 13 is not bankruptcy. In filing Chapter 13, you notify the U.S. Bankruptcy Court of your income and your debts. With their guidance, you create a monthly schedule to pay off all of your creditors gradually — over a period of no more than three years. The court may even arrange with your creditors for the reduction of some of your debts, holding you liable for, say, 50 cents on the dollar. A relatively routine procedure, there is rarely a need to hire a lawyer to protect your interests.

Once the court and your creditors have agreed to the plan, you are protected in the following ways:

- All legal action against you is stopped, and future action related to debts already incurred is prohibited.
- Your creditors are forbidden to contract your employer.
- Wage assignments and deductions cannot be made against you.
- A restraining order is issued by the courts to prevent your creditors from harassing you, or contacting you in any way.
- Late charges, service fees, and sometimes interest charges, are discontinued.

To file for Chapter 13, call the clerk of the nearest U.S. Bankruptcy Court. As the Court itself does not supply the forms, you'll be directed to a nearby legal stationer. The costs for filing are $60, plus a fee to a court-appointed trustee—amounting to ten percent of your monthly payments.

Should your debts become completely unmanageable, you can wipe them out by declaring bankruptcy. I don't advocate bankruptcy, but if you can't find another way to extricate yourself from your financial woes, you have a legal right to utilize it. According to a recent study, debts in the average bankruptcy total nine percent more than a person's annual income. Depending on the state you live in, you may be entitled to retain certain possessions after declaring bankruptcy.

The Clerk of the nearest Bankruptcy Court can tell you where to obtain the necessary forms. Fill them out, listing all of your debts and assets; debts not listed will not be discharged.

There are no two ways about it: Putting together a money plan is an out-and-out headache, which is why so few people ever do it. My first budgeting trial-by-fire began with my early corporate experience. Every quarter it was part of my job to submit a budget for my department for the forthcoming year. My budget requirements (the money my section needed) were then combined with the other departments' requirements so that top management could compute an overall corporate budget. Then the fun began—the rigorous chopping of outlay demanded by our profit projection.

I had to forecast what I was going to spend on advertising, sales promotion, flight transportation, hotels, conventions, and printing of brochures, as well as the salaries and commissions for the people in my department—all of which was, of course, to be subtracted from my sales forecast figures. Frankly, I hated every minute of it.

But it's absolutely essential—for people, not just for companies. How else can the money people know how much they need to support your plans, or what is required overall? And, almost as important, what simply can't be allowed? Maybe it all boils down to the fact that, in life as in business, there simply is no room for surprises that could have been anticipated. God knows, there are enough surprises that can't be planned for.

In the case of my private finances, after being clobbered with some unpleasant surprises — taxes, a big insurance premium, or some other out-of-the-blue bill — I began to realize that I could have planned for that "surprise" months in advance, which would have made its arrival a lot less painful. Its impact would have been reduced by pro-rating (and saving) the sum over those intervening months.

Take it from me, a money plan is vital to your financial liberation, and you might as well get started on it. Now.

It's part of the discipline process, too. The more involved you get, the sooner you can begin feeling better about your financial situation. It's like skiing. Those downhill racers look as though they're just wishing their way down the mountain, swooping and gliding along. Yet behind that seemingly effortless grace lie thousands of hours of hard practice and grueling training.

Some good news: For a money plan there are actually only two categories with which you need concern yourself. The first is your income, which should include salary and any other income you receive on a regular or periodic basis — stock dividends, alimony, annuity payments, and so on. Second is outflow, which includes fixed expenses such as rent or mortgage payments, utilities (heating, fuel, electricity, telephone, gas, water), insurance, loan payments, charge accounts, clothing, food, and so on. Plus savings. Yes. Place that in your outflow category, too — in order to ensure that you do set those amounts aside regularly.

Now for those big bills that come like thunderbolts here and there during the year, such as taxes, insurance premiums, school tuition, and vacations. They should be spread over twelve months rather than absorbed in one indigestible chunk in the week they occur. Let's take taxes as an example. Both income and property taxes can be estimated well in advance, either by referring to your last year's assessments or by getting the applicable tax tables from an accountant. All you need to do then is take that ump sum and divide it by twelve. For example, $1,560 divided by 12 = $130 a month (which looks a lot less frightening.) You then place that amount in each column-month. It should be kept in a money market or savings account.

What you're doing here is evening out the bumps (and shocks) by dealing with them on a monthly basis. A hundred dollars for an insurance premium twice a year may sting, but $16.60 per month is a breeze. And if you're worrying about where to get the figures for all of this, don't. You probably have all the information you need right there in your checkbook — rent or mortgage payments, department store bills, grocery checks, and so on. All you have to do is break them down into their various categories from the past year, tally them up, and you're off and running. By the way, your first effort at budgeting will probably be the most difficult; each year the process becomes easier and less time-consuming.

Now check your totals. Are you even? Or does your outflow exceed your income? If you're ahead, you may use that surplus as you see fit. If you're behind, you must cut back ruthlessly wherever you can. But don't simply tighten your belt. Get creative about your situation: Look around you, explore your possibilities, search for "hidden" money.

Look for items that can be converted into cash, such as old sports equipment, a painting you're tired of, furniture you no longer use, whatever. You might want to consider getting an extra job, or going after a raise in your current position. Also, call in any loans you may have made to friends or relatives.

To get yourself on the right fork in the road toward independence from money worries, you should take ten percent off the top and put it in a savings account, no matter what. That is going to make for still more belt-tightening at a time when you're also paying off your debts; but it is essential, not only as self-discipline but as a cushion against the unexpected.

Before placing your money in a savings account, it's wise to shop around. The competition among banks and savings and loan companies is so fierce that you should take advantage of it.

When determining which bank to use, you should be aware that the rates are constantly changing and will also vary from bank to bank. As you probably know, there are many different types of accounts, each of them carrying with it a set of government-established penalties, and so on. Always remember: Where savings are concerned, it's a buyer's market. That may be your only leverage. Use it wisely.

When shopping for bank accounts, you should ask the following questions (where applicable):

1. Cost per check on various kinds of accounts?
2. Monthly fees, if any?
3. Interest paid on checking accounts with specified minimum balance?
4. Minimum balance and charge for dropping below the minimum?
5. Free checking accounts available?
6. Overdraw account available to new customers? If so, at what rates of interest?
7. Cost for printed (personalized) checks in quantities of 250 or 500?
8. Other costs?
9. Bounced-check charge (overdraft)?
10. Stop payment charge?
11. Traveler's checks?
12. Safe Deposit Box?
13. Cashier's checks?
14. Certified checks?
15. Notary service?

Unless you're unemployed or cliff-hanging on the brink of total insolvency, you should be able to pay off your obligations within nine months. The first 90 days are the hardest, just as they are in sloughing excess fat from your body, but after that rather grim initial period you'll find there's a certain joy attached to self-discipline. Now you're down to muscle. And all the while you're ridding yourself of constant worry over bills and payments, you're also lightening your spirits because your bank account is growing steadily.

Your program of debt relief to enhance your financial picture will require certain tools.

Instead of that helter-skelter game you've been playing for so long, adopt a business-like procedure. Set aside an alcove, a small room, or at least the corner of a room for handling your financial affairs. Make that financial corner as attractive as possible, and keep a clear surface for working. Equip your corner with a good lamp, two file folders for paid and unpaid bills and another file for cancelled checks. Use manila folders for other documents and papers such as records of time payments on a car or appliances, receipts for tax-deductible items, W-2 forms, insurance forms. It's also important to select a certain day for meeting your monthly obligations. Most billings are sent out around the twenty-fifth; I've found it's a good idea to set aside a particular, regular day between the first and tenth of the succeeding month to make out checks and mail them off.

A friend of mine, who used these very steps to climb out of debt, has equipped a room in her house like a small office, complete with desk, four-drawer filing cabinet, fresh flowers to cheer her flagging will and her indispensible electronic calculator. She refers to it as "the room" — and she now runs her successful real estate ventures and other investments from it. She has also collected and developed a fairly comprehensive investment library, which is housed there.

A successful and effective life is the result of productive

habits made second nature; perhaps the most necessary habit to encourage is constant awareness of outflow as well as income.

Obviously your financial base will not be broadened unless you can consciously hold the outflow down as much as possible, especially during periods of inflation. The habit of comparative pricing will take you much farther than blindly scrimping, reducing yourself to a bare subsistence level.

The success of your personal economy will depend on the intelligence with which you buy the things you need. You must learn to think of yourself as a company purchasing agent, charged with keeping the cost of everything—from office supplies to the output of the coffee machine—as low as possible.

All right. You've gone, say, nine months on the money diet, and you've settled a lot of things. You've proved yourself responsible, your saving habit has now became ingrained, and you know that an unforeseen doctor's bill won't throw your new life-style out of gear. You shouldn't need a crash diet again. Now it's a question of holding the line and keeping in shape. You understand the bone and sinew of your own financial structure. You're ready to step out now with brand-new confidence. You're ready to establish a sound credit position and begin evaluating the various elements of your financial foundation including savings, real estate, stocks and much more. You're ready to be creative and positive instead of negative.

4

Women and Credit

I have long believed the most important law ever passed for women was the Equal Credit Opportunity Act.

While millions lament the fact that the Equal Rights Amendment was not passed, it is more important to focus on what *was* passed. The Equal Credit Opportunity Act went a great distance in giving us legal equality with men. And that equality doesn't mean just credit cards; it includes lines of credit, venture capital and real estate loans.

In my estimation, one of the most vital components of your financial success portfolio is solid credit. That means, initially, getting it established, building it up over a period of time and, finally, using and leveraging your credit when you need it — to buy a home, finance a new company, or borrow to fund your IRA. Whatever your purpose, having solid credit is part of the joy of money — and the joy of being a complete and prosperous human being.

Establishing credit can be a challenging, and sometimes frustrating, undertaking. But if you view it as a necessary goal — one which will reap rewards later and open doors when you need them most — your achievement of that goal will bring you a great deal of satisfaction. As with most of life's ventures, there are "rules of the road"; you'll need to know them before you get started, and follow them once you've begun.

"Women," it has been said, "don't get the credit they deserve — in more ways than one." It's common knowledge that until recently, women were second-class citizens when it came to acquiring general credit cards and, more importantly, bank loans and mortgages. Department stores have long recognized the purchasing power of women, and have been less reluctant to grant us credit than commercial institutions. But in the more critical, long-term credit areas — getting real estate or business loans — we were still viewed as flighty, lacking determination and seriousness and, as Lord Chesterfield put it so quaintly, "below men and above children."

Thanks to the Equal Credit Opportunity Act, the picture has changed dramatically. A woman applying for credit can, for the most part, expect to be treated in the same manner as her male counterpart . . . if she follows the same strategy.

Before you fill out that first application, you've got to know what creditors look for. In a word, it's creditworthiness, or what that venerable publication, "The Banker's Handbook," refers to as "the three C's of credit" — character, capital and capacity. Simply put, it means "Does the person pay? Can the person pay? Will the person pay?" The criteria are essentially standard, regardless of the type of credit you're seeking. Creditors generally consider the following factors in determining your ability, and willingness, to pay your debts:

Age: Typically, you must be at least 18 — the age at which you're legally bound to honor a contract — in most states.

Stability: In determining your stability, a creditor will look at how long you've lived in a certain area (and at your current address), whether you rent or own your home, and whether you have savings, insurance or investments.

Income: You can expect to be asked to provide information regarding your occupation and employer: how long you've worked at your present job, how much you earn and how you're compensated (salary, commission, fee). Many creditors will also want to know whether you have other sources of income, such as pensions, profit-sharing plans or dividends. By law, you're not required to disclose in your application any income from alimony, child support or separate maintenance agreements — unless you want a potential creditor to consider this income.

Expenses: Obviously, the ratio of your income to your fixed expenses influences your ability to pay your debts. At the very least, you'll probably be asked to reveal the number of your dependents, and your financial obligations.

Debt Record: A potential creditor will look at how much you already owe and, more importantly, how promptly you pay your bills. They may ask how often you borrow, and for what purposes. They will also want to know whether any of your accounts have ever gone to collection; whether you've had an item purchased on credit repossessed; and if you've ever declared bankruptcy.

A lesson I've learned over the years in filling out credit applications, is to avoid doing so at the bank or credit institution. It's much more difficult to supply information in a complete and correct fashion if you feel you're under pressure. Take them home, or to your office, for completion, and always make a photocopy of the applications (as well as any other forms you may fill out).

In addition to the information you supply on your application, a potential creditor will probably also request your file from a credit reporting agency, if only to verify the information you've already supplied. For that reason, it's *crucial* that you provide correct information; a creditor can deny your request if your figures can't be backed up, or if you've withheld pertinent information.

It's probably a good idea to request a copy of your credit report *before* you apply for new credit. Some of the larger bureaus have offices nationwide, but if you can't decide which one to use after consulting the Yellow Pages, call a major bank or department store in your area and find out which one they use. There's a small fee, usually $6-$10, and you'll need to supply information such as your date and place of birth, your current address, your driver's license number and Social Security number. By doing this, you can make certain beforehand that the report presents an accurate picture of your credit history, and can arrange to have any incorrect information deleted. Also, if you have a dispute with a creditor about an item or payment, you can request that the dispute be entered into your report.

Once you've done your homework, and filled out applications, the ball moves into the creditor's court. How will they decide? If your application checks out, and your credit report shows a good repayment history, it's virtually guaranteed you'll get credit, up to the limit the creditor figures you can repay. If you don't have a credit file — or if it's insufficient — a creditor may use a credit scoring system. Your score will be determined by characteristics such as income, length of employment, how long you've lived in your present address, among others. If you're going to be evaluated according to the credit scoring system, I suggest you plead your case *in person*. We're all human, and a potential creditor is sure to be more easily persuaded by your earnest, straightforward manner (backed up by a typed itemization of your income and monetary commitments), than by a few sheets of paper placed in his or her "in" box. The following chart gives you an idea of how your creditworthiness will be determined.

Marital status: Married, add one point.

Dependents: One to three, add two points; four or more, add one point.

Age: 21-25, add one point; 26-64, add two points; over 65, add one point.

Residence: Over five years at same address, add one point.

Job status: Less than one year at present job, add no points; one to three years, add one point; four to six years, add two points; seven to ten years, add three points; over ten years, add four points.

Monthly obligations: Less than $200, add one point; over $200, add no points.

Type of work: If you are in one of the professions, an executive or foreman, add three points; skilled worker, add two points; blue-collar worker, add one point; anything else, add no points.

Loans: If you have a loan at the bank where you are applying for credit, add five points; if you have loan experience at another bank or finance company, add three points.

Bank accounts: If you have a checking or savings account at the bank where you are applying for credit, add two points.

Telephone: Listed in your name, add two points.

Getting Started — Some Practical Steps To Take

Whether you're establishing credit for the first time, or getting your feet back on the ground after a divorce, you'll need to develop, and play out, your strongest suit. And that suit will *always* include a good, and personal, relationship with your local banker. I'm not talking about the pleasant young man behind the teller's window. The point here is that you've got to establish a rapport with someone who has power, preferably a manager or assistant manager, even if your initial intentions are only to open a checking and/or savings account. You'll find that, in establishing or adding to your credit, those accounts — backed up by your personal relationship with a top bank officer — will be your most valuable asset. Once you've set up those accounts, maintain them responsibly, as potential creditors view your handling of them as a prime indicator of your good money management habits.

Apply for credit in your community initially. Creditors doing business in your area are more likely to know you or your employer, and facts on your credit application can be readily verified from local sources. If you're new to the area, find out whether you have a credit report with an agency in your former area, and arrange to have it transferred. You may have to pay a small fee, but if it's all the armor you have, you'll need it.

Speaking of armor, use everything you can get your hands on. If you're new to the game, it's no time to get out your combat boots and march for women's rights. The issue here is plain and simple — to get the credit you need. Even though I strongly advise that married women establish credit in their own names (more on this later), if you need to use your spouse's salary or cosignature to get credit, do so. Find your sources of leverage and use them. This may mean a personal introduction from your accountant, financial advisor, employer, preferably someone who has a vested interest (ideally someone who is already doing business with the bank or institution) — anyone who's willing to say that you're reputable and creditworthy.

As I've said before, the personal approach is *always* the most effective one. Few people realize that a bank manager can personally sign off on a Visa or MasterCard (even if you have no credit or a married credit rating). And he or she is going to do that based on the impression you make. Be as businesslike as possible; stress the positive aspects of your income potential and career growth possibilities; and, of course, your intentions to manage your credit wisely.

Credit Discrimination

Fortunately, since the passing of the Equal Credit Opportunity Act, incidences of discrimination in granting credit to women have become very rare. Creditors are willingly complying with the law, if only because the penalties for not doing so can be substantial. Besides, competition among creditors has become very fierce indeed, and creditors, like anyone involved in consumer goods and services, aren't going to invite the bad press a discrimination lawsuit might bring.

Regardless of the protection afforded by the Equal Credit Opportunity Act, instances of discrimination can, and do, occur. The victims, ironically, are often married women, who still face the dilemma of being judged by their husbands' credit histories, regardless of whether the spouse's credit rating reflects her own credit history or earning ability.

Take the recent case of Patricia Brothers, who submitted an application to lease a car from First Leasing Corporation. She had a good job, a substantial salary, and a sterling credit history. In spite of the fact that she, personally, met the necessary requirements for obtaining the lease, Ms. Brothers was turned down because her husband had once declared bankruptcy.

She sued for discrimination under the ECOA, but her suit was thrown out of the U.S. Federal Court. She appealed to the U.S. Court of Appeals, who overturned the initial decision and came out strongly in favor of individual credit evaluation. The subsequent ruling also disallowed discrimination in the charging of higher fees and interest rates to women.

Although Ms. Brothers' story had a happy ending, and ramifications for all of us in the arena of obtaining personal credit, women in business continue to battle bias in commercial lending practices. Although the ECOA forbids lenders from asking personal questions about a woman's marital status or her family planning intentions, that practice is still prevalent among commercial creditors.

Ann Stone, who runs a successful $15-million direct-mail business in Alexandria, VA, found herself up against a wall when she asked her bank for a $25,000 line of credit. The bank officers wanted her husband's co-signature to make the loan to a company he owned no part of. Ms. Stone's experience is not unique. Thelma Ablan, owner of Castle Construction Co., had $1 million worth of business on her books when she approached her bank for a $50,000 line of credit. She received the sum, but only after her husband signed the application.

An even more distressing scenario was the one faced by Anna Filomena when she sought funds to start a new restaurant three years ago. Lenders repeatedly asked her what would happen to the restaurant if she got married. Although she insisted it would make no difference, her requests for loans continued to be denied. Although she finally received a $550,000 loan guarantee from the Small Business Administration, and business at her chic Georgetown restaurant is booming, she still harbors resentment about the obvious discrimination. "I don't know of any man who presents a business package and is asked, 'What's going to happen if you get married?'" she says.

A bill recently introduced to the House of Representatives proposes that lenders be required to treat both business and consumer loans in the same way. This effort to amend the ECOA is one of several developments in the campaign to add marital status to the factors that cannot legally affect business decisions and lending practices.

Obviously, these issues won't be resolved overnight. It's important, then, to use the laws that are in effect now, if you feel you've been discriminated against. Here's a suggested course of action:

1. Ask for a *written* explanation of why you have been denied credit.
2. Keep detailed records of your attempts to convince

creditors of your worthiness and need for equity.

3. Contact the Federal Trade Commission, and the U.S. Attorney General's office, and explain your situation, describing any action taken to date.

4. If you still get no satisfaction, you can start proceedings to file a suit against the lender(s). Contact an attorney with experience in discrimination cases. If you can't get a personal reference for one, the American Bar Association can provide you with a list of local attorneys with this expertise.

Credit Reporting — The Rules of the Game

According to Delia Fernandez, Director of Public Affairs for TRW, one of the country's largest credit reporting companies, women *are* generally treated equally when it comes to receiving personal credit. She allows, however, that women tend still to have misconceptions about the factors involved in qualifying for credit. "Many women don't realize that they are subject to the same set of criteria as men when it comes to applying for credit," says Delia. "They think somehow that the new law means they will automatically be granted credit — that it's some kind of a *carte blanche*. Women fail to realize that if their income is insufficient, or if they fail to meet a creditor's standards in other areas, there's a good possibility they'll be denied credit." She cites the example of a woman who, with an annual income of $6000, applied for a loan for a $15,000 car. When she failed to get the loan, she thought she'd been discriminated against simply because she was a woman. It's obvious, with even minor calculations, that anyone in that income bracket would have difficulty making payments amounting to such a large percentage of their net income.

Ms. Fernandez also maintains that women going through a

divorce often fail to realize the implications for their personal credit. It's not the divorce itself, but the lack of planning and foresight that places women in a credit bind. "Establishing credit *during* a marriage is essential," she says, "because you're going to have a tough time getting credit after a divorce when you haven't established a personal credit history, and when, as it often happens, your income is significantly lower than your spouse's."

Another surprising—and shockingly prevalent—problem is that women going through a divorce are often advised to hold off on payments on joint accounts until a judge approves a financial settlement. "Women are often unaware that, regardless of who is ultimately held accountable for certain debts, their personal liability remains as long as the account was a joint one. And a 30- or 60-day late payment can have a detrimental effect on anyone's credit rating," says Fernandez. She suggests that one way to avoid potential problems is to request to have your name taken off a joint account for which you will no longer be liable. A more drastic measure, which should be considered when there is bitter conflict over a settlement, is to close down all joint accounts, if possible.

Managing Your Credit

Let's assume you've done your homework, gotten over a few hurdles and managed to establish some credit. What you have to deal with now is your attitude toward credit. Used intelligently and wisely, credit will help you build your future. Think of credit as a tool—one of the most important tools you'll ever have to work with—not as a one-way ticket to a long fantasized spending spree. Your wise management of credit cards and continued demonstration of your credit worthiness will be your means of obtaining long-term credit when you need it—to start a business, invest in real estate, or take part in some other potentially lucrative venture.

Credit abuse has reached almost epidemic proportions in this country. According to Donna Fong, Director of Consumer Credit Counselors in Los Angeles, the 25-to-35 set, singles or couples, are the consumers most likely to get into trouble with credit cards. Regardless of the fact that they're well educated, make decent incomes and think they "have their act together," Ms. Fong says, many young people find themselves deep into credit card debt in a very short time. A typical client, she says, is the young person who suddenly finds that their short-term debt liability exceeds 35 percent of their annual income, and they've reached the point of not even being able to meet the monthly minimum payments on their accounts.

The culprit is most often that time-worn, and yet timeless, compulsion to "keep up with the Joneses." In our fashion-conscious society designer clothing and dining in trendy, $100-dinner-for-two restaurants are *de rigeur*. Many young people, says Ms. Fong, have no realistic conception of their actual spending power.

If you think you're a prime candidate for overspending, your best course is probably to limit yourself to the essentials: one bank card (Visa or MasterCard), one department store card, and one gasoline company card. And try, whenever possible, to pay your balance in full each month. Sometimes, of course, it makes sense to charge a major purchase such as an appliance or item of furniture, when it's being offered at a substantial discount. If you figure the interest you'll pay in the long run still makes the purchase a bargain, it might be a good move.

What To Do If Your Debts Pile Up

If you find that you're sinking into a morass of unpaid bills, resist the urge to stuff those late notices in the back of your desk drawer. Face the music, and take action. Immediately. The first step is to find out where you stand, by preparing a Personal Financial Statement. (See Chapter 3.) The next step is to figure out whether you can whittle down your debt load by cutting back on other expenses. If you haven't been keeping track of where your money goes, use the information in your financial statement to prepare a budget.

Set some specific, short-term goals, such as bringing your loan payments up to date as soon as possible. And resolve *not* to take on any more debts. In some cases, paring your spending and monitoring your finances may be all you need to get back on track. You may find, though, that these measures aren't going to cut the cake. If that's the case, it's time to talk to your creditors.

Don't worry initially about what kind of reception you'll get. Most creditors will appreciate your straightforward approach, especially if you've paid your bills regularly in the past. Go prepared with budget in hand — and be honest about the reason for your financial bind, whether it's because you've run up large medical bills, lost your job, or just overextended yourself.

Creditors generally handle payment problems on a case-by-case basis, taking into account the type of loan, your financial situation, and payment history. They may offer you an extension of, say, 30 or 60 days; or offer to rewrite your loan for a longer period of time.

If you aren't able to arrange a mutually acceptable scheme with your creditors, you may want to consider a debt-consolidation loan or financial counseling. The problem with debt-consolidation loans is you usually end up paying a higher rate of interest than you were paying on the charge card accounts. Being able to pay off your debts over a longer period of time takes away some stress. It also simplifies your life in that you have only one bill to pay each month, but there's a price tag attached, and those additional interest charges can be substantial. Another potential problem with consolidation loans is that if you haven't made a commitment to treat the illness, you may end up just relieving the symptoms—temporarily. All too often, someone gets the consolidation loan and, in short order, gets more credit, beginning the process all over again.

If you have the courage to admit that you're a "credit junkie," a better alternative might be to seek counseling. Consumer Credit Counselors, a government-sponsored, non-profit agency, provides free advice on debt management. If your situation merits more than just advice on budgeting and billpaying, you can enroll in their cooperative debt management program. For a nominal fee, they'll devise a workable plan with your creditors, usually over a three-year period. To find the nearest office, write or call: The National Foundation for Consumer Credit, 8701 Georgia Avenue, Silver Spring, MD 20910. (301) 589-5600.

As a note of caution, beware of "Credit Clinics" not affiliated with the NFCC. Although they promise the same type of service, many have unethical practices. You may end up paying, up front, for services promised but never received.

Charging Smart

In acquiring credit, as in making purchases, it pays to be a smart shopper. Increased competition among banks and credit granting institutions gives you more options than ever, including some very attractive new choices on credit cards—reduced annual fees and variable interest rates, for example. Even if you've already acquired your credit card portfolio, take a good look at it to make sure that you've chosen the cards that work best for your budgeting and borrowing needs. Check out how much interest you're paying; rates can vary from a low of 12.5 percent annually at one company, to 24 percent at another. One company, Avco National Bank (800-524-6000) even offers a no-fee credit card. The only requirements are that you have a gross monthly income of $1200 and two credit cards you've been using for two years or more.

To find the best value in credit cards, contact BankCard Holders of America, 303 Pennsylvania Avenue, S.E., Washington, D.C. (202)543-5805).

5

On Your Own:
Becoming An Entrepreneur

This subject is close to my heart since it's the path I and many enterprising women have chosen in moving from nine-to-five routines into entrepreneurial ventures that have proved lively, fulfilling and profitable. When I started working, I never dreamed I would have my own company, and I'm reasonably sure that other women to whom you'll be introduced in this book didn't either—not until they'd spent several years on corporate ladders or in institutional corridors and then, for one reason or another, got the entrepreneurial "bug."

Take the case of Stephanie Winston, a former book editor who decided to turn her propensity for neatness and organization to her advantage. She left publishing, wrote a book on her area of expertise and formed her own service company. She now counsels some of the industrial giants like IBM and Xerox on how to improve their filing systems—and even individuals such as doctors and other professionals who need help in straightening out the confusion in their offices. And then there's Barbara Boyle

Sullivan, an ex-IBM executive who became so successful at running their women's affirmative action program that she formed Boyle/Kirkman Associates, which specializes in helping executives establish fair employment practices in their own firms—a creative spin-off indeed.

The most exciting thing about running your own company (either by yourself or with a partner) is that it is something you can love wholeheartedly, throw all your energies into: it's your baby. It can also be your prime investment vehicle, as it is in my own case.

Even if you're not interested in this route to self-realization today, don't write it off. You may be in the future. Meanwhile, if you're somewhere deep in the corporate structure, you're learning a lot of valuable things about company organization, personnel, marketing—all the ingredients that make up the corporate pudding.

For me, launching your own business is like writing your own personal declaration of independence from the corporate beehive, where you sell bits of your life in forty-hour (or longer) chunks in return for a paycheck. Having participated in the founding of more than six new business concerns, I've discovered it's far more rewarding, both emotionally and financially, to work twice as long at something you've conceived and nurtured. Of course, let's face it, entrepreneurship has its frustrations, even its downright terrifying moments. There have been times when Webster's definition of the entrepreneur as undertaker can take on rather grim overtones. It's true, you may be risking all that time and effort for nothing, but the potential rewards are worth it. There are times when I honestly think I'd rather own a pizza parlor than be one of a herd of vice-presidents in some mammoth corporation.

Going into business for yourself, becoming an entrepreneur, is the modern-day equivalent of pioneering on the old frontier. There are dangers, make no mistake about that; but there are just as many opportunities and they are virtually as limitless as they are unique and exciting. The last two decades have been hailed as the new age of the entrepreneur, which most experts feel has come about as a reaction to the bigness, the impersonal steam-roller quality of corporate life, too monolithic to allow exploitation of the small opportunities that can be seized by one person or by a small and enterprising group.

Almost everyone, male or female, has a natural timidity about striking out alone, about giving up the security of a job in exchange for independence, trading the known for the unknown. After all, there are distinct and undeniable advantages to working for a large organization. The abundant resources and sophisticated support systems of corporations contribute largely to their success — particularly if the industry is a complex one. In spite of these relative "comforts," the enticing notion of starting one's own business captivates a would-be entrepreneur, who is willing to cope with risk in search of greater rewards.

For the woman with entrepreneurial aspirations, it's time to press outward from the traditional fields in which it was generally conceded that women might excel simply because they were women.

We all know how Elizabeth Arden and Helena Rubenstein achieved resounding success in the cosmetics industry. Now, however, women are expanding into less traditional areas. They are heading companies — and succeeding — as computer consultants, manufacturers, developers and engineers, as well as in the more traditional roles of interior decorating and public relations.

Others are joining together to form new businesses connected with banking, credit, publishing and sports. Women now own nearly 25 percent of the 13 million small businesses in the country, and that percentage is on the rise. An astounding three times as many women are starting businesses as men.

What Does It Take?

Entrepreneurs hold a fascination for everyone, even other entrepreneurs. In the last 30 years, researchers have produced endless studies in an attempt to answer the question, "What does it take to be an entrepreneur?" The general consensus is that the issue isn't as ambiguous as one might think. There's considerable diversity in the external factors—industry, location, capital invested, family background—but the personality traits among successful entrepreneurs are essentially shared.

As general as it might sound, the most common trait among entrepreneurs is a high need for achievement—*personal* achievement.

Surprisingly enough, a successful entrepreneur tends to prefer an *intermediate* level of risk, a finding which clearly contradicts the popular notion that entrepreneurs are "high-rolling risk-takers." Obviously, taking risk is part of the fun, but achieving the goal is the primary motivator.

Entrepreneurs have an insatiable craving for unambiguous and timely feedback; and prefer situations which allow for innovative and novel solutions.

Finally, most entrepreneurs have a strong future orientation. They look for ventures which require a great deal of planning, presumably feeding their anticipation of future possibilities.

A fascinating aspect of the theory about entrepreneurs is the part that money plays in the motivation process. Money, in and of itself, doesn't directly motivate the "classic" entrepreneur. Instead, money is a barometer, a source of feedback—for the extent of the entrepreneur's achievement. Obviously, money is important to the entrepreneur—as a means and an end—but in the long run it's the need for achievement that takes precedence over the desire for monetary reward.

In weighing the risks of entering the marketplace on your own, you should take a long, hard look at your motivations for making such a move. Some of you may have the requisite ambition but not the special talents or instincts of an entrepreneur. Others may possess the mental and emotional equipment and still not welcome the total unflagging commitment that having your own company involves.

Nor is everyone cut out to be boss, especially boss of a fledgling outfit. This is a question you must examine with ruthless objectivity. For instance, you may find that your strong suit is implementing decisions already made—in which case the entrepreneur's gambit is not for you.

Or you may discover that your strength lies in functioning as part of a team; in that case, you need to find a partner who is endowed with those skills you yourself lack or are not interested in developing.

If you do decide to go into a business partnership with someone, the only way you can truly evaluate a potential leader of a young and therefore highly risky venture is to ask for an extensive biography of the person involved—and then do a little quiet checking on your own. If your prospective partner is the real thing, he or she will have no qualms about your checking, and that includes making a few telephone calls to previous or current associates as well as former employers. To put it crudely, don't be snowed or dazzled by the glitter of talent. Once you've checked the biography and made your queries, the glitter may prove to be duller or even decidedly tarnished. And if a prospective collaborator stalls about giving you a biography, or refuses outright to give you one, drop the whole thing immediately.

My own experience in the area of joint enterprise was a very happy one. Beyond the exceptional imagination and drive that I could recognize for myself, my first partner had a superlative track record. Nonetheless, you can be sure that I did some research before making a final decision. You are investing a sizable chunk of your life in any new venture, and it behooves you to bring to the selection all the care and caution you would display in choosing a surgeon to perform a serious operation. The life you lose may be your own.

Your next step is to examine, every bit as impersonally, your reasons for leaving your present berth. They will tell you a lot about your capacity for striking out on your own. (Often the main reason is simple discontent.) You should run down the following possible motives for being dissatisfied as someone else's employee — dispose of the negative aspects of your projected move before shifting to the positive side of the ledger.

As a corporate employee, do you feel that there is a considerable gap between what you contribute to your employer's financial success and the rewards and compensation you receive? Few companies, from my experience and that of many people with whom I've talked, are equipped to compensate fairly the truly creative people on their payroll. They may pay bonuses, say, for patents-applied-for in their research laboratories, but the reward system is often based on the number rather than the commercial worth of such patents. A diligent and imaginative innovator can find herself ranked below mediocre hirelings who produce in quantity rather than quality.

Take the case of Evelyn Berezin, who had a Ph.D. in physics and worked for other companies for years while making important contributions in the data processing field. Despite her inventive genius, she found that her sex was a severe handicap in achieving executive status.

"I could do a better job than most of the people around me," she said, "yet I could see that I was never going to get any further as an employee."

This, despite the fact that she was an early arrival in the computer industry and had started out by designing computers for a small company in New York; and later, while employed by a Connecticut firm, developed the first nationwide reservations system for United Air Lines.

Along the way she abandoned her struggle to persuade the corporate brass that she deserved a better shake, and with $375,000 in borrowed capital plus a very promising idea she founded Redactron Corporation on Long Island.

"I was convinced," she explained, "that something could be done to improve productivity by applying the computer to secretarial work.

She then proceeded, along with three colleagues, to design an editing-typewriter system that produced typewritten copies of an original letter or document that had been recorded on a magnetic tape cassette. It was a field pioneered by IBM; Redactron was merely one of many smaller companies competing in the million-dollar market.

Dr. Berezin put in 14-hour days while mounting her challenge to the IBM empire. For several years Redactron's balance sheets were inscribed in red ink. One year the company lost $2.5 million on revenues of only $1.8 million. Sales then increased to an impressive $7 million annually and Redactron turned the corner when Sperry Rand's prestigious Remington Rand division contracted to buy $3.4 million worth of Redactron systems and sell them under the Remington Rand label.

Forming her own company, she said, was the only way she could fully capitalize on her talent and training. It took courage and initiative to step out of a well-paying job when she had just turned forty. But today she has not only the satisfaction of success, but the far deeper gratification of having won it on her own.

If you're a creative innovator who is disappointed in the way you've been rewarded, starting your own concern is worth the effort and risk, provided you can secure the marketing and financial expertise to match your abilities. But be honest with yourself. Many people simply can't function without the resources of a large corporation behind them. This is an important point for you to weigh. An astounding number of bankruptcies result from big-company-type spending by infant firms. Recent statistics on new business start-ups and failures suggest that the entrepreneur faces a greater threat to survival than the nearly extinct peregrine falcon. Although estimates conflict, it appears that roughly one-third of all new businesses fail within twelve months, and that rate increases to one-half by the end of the third year.

Are you dissatisfied with your rate of promotion or your company's promotion policies? Many people feel that they are kept in one position too long—and often enough they are—because those with seniority are largely preoccupied with keeping them on a lower rung of the corporate ladder, as a protection against losing their own status. This is particularly true of firms that do not have automatic retirement ceilings, where one aging owner or partner can destroy irreparably a firm's future by selfishly keeping out younger business talent.

Are you being defeated by office politics or by your company's practice of giving the plums to relatives? Many concerns are rife with water-cooler plots and corridor politicking. Some of the smaller firms are operated by members of one family, and non-kinfolk find the key executive spots closed to them.

Are you being stifled by a proliferation of red tape? Many companies are run like government bureaucracies and tend to manufacture as much needless paperwork as the products they are set up to make and market. There's nothing more frustrating to a woman with initiative than having to deal with people who insulate their own inadequacies and avoid decision-making with layers of red tape.

Are you being held back by educational snobbery? Many corporations are more interested in the degrees you've acquired, however intrinsically worthless or irrelevant they may be to job requirements, than in your real capacities. If you don't have a college degree, no matter how bright and ambitious you are, you'll find the avenues to advancement blocked at this kind of firm. Even if you do have the degree, you may find it inhibits your advancement because it isn't from the "right" school. You may be pounding your head against the Ivy League wall.

All these reasons are valid enough to fire your discontent with working for an employer who can't or won't perceive true excellence, no matter what its guise. They don't necessarily qualify you, though, to start your own business. They are negative arguments — and may merely signify that you should change passage on ocean liners, not take the helm of your own sloop.

If you feel you have more positive qualifications for going into business on your own, you should submit yourself to still another frank and candid self-assessment. Your own character is vital to such a new venture as any brilliant ideas you may have for staking out your own clearing in the woods.

Before taking the plunge, give strong consideration to the following positive factors:

1. *DRIVE.* You must possess a built-in self-starting mechanism. You aren't the type that needs to be pushed into action swiftly and decisively. You should have a compulsion for hard work and late hours. You must be willing, even eager, to sacrifice your spare time, sports interests and social life.

2. *EXECUTIVE COMPETENCE.* You must have an exceptional capacity for gathering relevant information, deciding what is accurate and applicable, and acting on it. More often than not you must work with incomplete information, and chart the best course just the same. The fear of making a mistake, resulting in failure to act decisively, has ended many a budding venture. You have to be able to act decisively and take the consequences: The buck, truly, does stop here.

3. *MOTIVATION.* You've got to *want* success, to struggle unremittingly for it — and you must be resilient enough to bounce back from the setbacks, frustrations, or defeats that accompany most new ventures. You must be prepared to look upon your fledgling company as a child to be reared. It will take incessant care and thought; its nurturing and feeding can be a round-the-clock proposition. Many people simply cannot get that involved in something that seems to lack a personality. To the true entrepreneur, however, her company does have a personality, a marvelous life of its own that she has breathed into it.

4. *EXPERTISE.* You must immerse yourself in the product

or service you're offering the market. You must know it inside and out — its strengths and its weaknesses, its potential and pitfalls — and you must know them better than anyone else. You may think you can learn as you go, and profit from mistakes made through ignorance, but few emerging entrepreneurs have the capital to afford that sort of on-the-job training. The clock ticks very fast in the business world, and the tuition fee demanded by the school of hard knocks can wipe you out before you're fairly started. Far better to have mastered the field you're planning to invade as an employee, privy to the trade secrets and methods of operation of someone already familiar with the field. That way you can acquire the requisite expertise before you launch your own canoe into the rapids.

5. *LEADERSHIP.* You must — absolutely must — possess what can only be called leadership: that rare-as-rubies personal force that can resolve the clash of issues and personalities, pull others along with you and induce them to see things your way. You must inspire subordinates through example — working an hour or two longer than anyone else, having an answer when no one else does. Yes, there will be times when you have to simulate assurance, even when your own stomach is full of butterflies. In short, you have to inspire confidence and emulation 24 hours a day — or so it seems. All too often the chief of some new enterprise discovers at the moment of crunch that she lacks the ultimate clout or persuasiveness to forge a unanimity of view, and is forced to watch her fledgling company come apart at the seams.

6. *MANAGERIAL ACUMEN.* You should be a shrewd judge of character. You must be able to appraise the qualifications of prospective associates and lieutenants in the close personnel terms of your new venture. You must be able to winnow avarice from ambition, flattery from loyalty, reflectiveness from lack of fiber. If you're entering into a partnership, your skills should dovetail, and your personality complement your partner's. Incompatible natures are fatal to a new business. You must

analyze and measure the strengths and weaknesses of your prospective associates and you must have the courage to obey that small inner voice if it murmurs to you that something in the personal equation is radically wrong.

7. *SENSE OF PERFECTION.* Finally, you should have an abiding contempt for the mediocre, the easy road, the gold brick; a boundless and inexorable sense of the possible beyond the impossible — that deep interior excitement at the challenge you throw in your own path, an all-consuming need to be the best you can be. Happiness is competence perfectly fulfilled.

These qualities are musts for any budding entrepreneur, and you'd better make sure you have most or all of them. A few of them can be learned, it's true, but the genuine entrepreneur feels them deeply without thinking about them. They are the thrust, the life force, that drives her.

A proud possessor of all these qualities and a ringing inspiration to us all is Ruth Houghton Axe, who cut through the corporate jungle like a newly honed machete some years ago. Talk about your Renaissance man — this small, dynamic lady not only mastered her share of the business world but played the cello, excelled at chess, and was a crack shot with a rifle. (On one occasion she hit every target in a shooting gallery.)

She was an employee of the New York Telephone Company when she married Emerson Axe, a securities analyst for the same firm. Undoubtedly the work she did for Ma Bell trained her to research a subject thoroughly — a skill that she was to stand her in good stead in later years, when she would make herself an expert on any company she investigated, an authority who couldn't be fooled by a tricky balance sheet or an overly optimistic annual report.

But her impatience with the ponderous corporation was all her own. She wanted, as she said, to run her own shop. She persuaded her husband, a quiet, amiable, low-keyed man, to leave New York Telephone and branch out with her as an investment counsel team (Axe-Houghton Financial Services), then on to mutual funds and industrial ventures. Emerson Axe was an excellent securities analyst in his own right, but Ruth was the emotional mainspring of their enterprises.

The valuable lesson of her career is that it was founded not simply on a dynamic personality—though she had that to spare—but on the incredible preparation she underwent before she made any important move. Homework was the key to her success in carving any new trail of opportunity. She would stay up half the night reading up on and analyzing some venture before Axe-Houghton took any part of its development. She made herself an expert on liquid fertilizers, for example, realizing their crucial importance to agricultural production—before most people had ever heard of them. She acquired expertise, and startled the specialists, in such esoteric fields as mercury mining. She even went down into the mines herself. She mastered the history and chemistry of cement construction; she went into the field and analyzed the possibilities of lava-based cement, which is lighter than Portland cement and therefore cheaper to transport.

Ruth Axe was always willing to take a gamble, associates will tell you, but she never risked a flyer until she had informed herself on every aspect of the venture. And she had a healthy contempt for evasive rhetoric. Small, combative, with a volatile temperament and a furious impatience with anyone who tried to outfox her, she developed an uncanny ability to penetrate the heart of any matter.

A sales executive who knew her well told me, "She ran the outfit like a candy store." He meant it as a compliment, in the sense that she made it her business to know every detail of the operations under a corporate umbrella better than any of the managers of the companies involved. She would write a check for a million dollars without flinching, but she went around switching off the lights in the offices at night (she was often the last to shut up shop) to cut down overhead. There is nothing ironic about this; she knew all too well, as any business chief of mission does, that profit margins are eroded by a vast array of small-leakage expenses.

I've given this mini-biography of Ruth Axe in detail because it highlights so beautifully the strategy any woman must devise and follow if she wants to clamber out of the wage-earning ranks. Her career is an entrepreneur's dream. She had determined at the earliest stages that she was not to be satisfied with a desk, a comfortable salary and a pension from Ma Bell; she was determined to use her hard-won abilities for her own benefit. She knew the incomparable value of homework, and she could drive herself harder and longer than most people. She accepted the sacrifices involved: Her companies were her "children," and she gave them requisite loving care. She saw that her talents and Emerson's complemented each other—his lay in analysis, hers in acquisitions and sales—and that their temperaments didn't clash. She mastered the expertise that gave her unquestioned authority in board meetings. She was not afraid to take large risks. And she had that compelling need for achievement, for perfection in her own world. Consequently, she won all the marbles.

As I've mentioned before, entrepreneurs aren't necessarily fortune-seekers. What the true entrepreneur possesses is an energetic belief in her most cherished scheme. That's why it's so important to focus on your specialty, or field of knowledge, and use it to launch your venture. A recent story in *Business Week* listed several types of businesses in which '80s entrepreneurs had made substantial fortunes. One of them was the dry-cleaning industry. You can bet that in the next twelve months, a substantial number of would-be entrepreneurs will go out and rent storefronts, set up shop and wait for the bucks to come rolling in. If you don't know anything about dry-cleaning and, worse yet, don't *care* about it, chances are you wouldn't be successful.

The point is to start with what you know best. Empires are built on bright ideas, but you've got to *believe* in that bright idea. Take Joan Barnes, who in 1976 was earning $5000 a year working part-time in a community center children's program. Ten years later, she's still looking after toddlers, but she's now worth over $1 million, and her company, Gymboree, grossed over $5 million in 1984.

A true entrepreneur, Joan had a sound idea for a business in a field she loved. In her now nationwide program, toddlers learn to jump, tumble, slide, interact with other children—and play a variety of educational games. Joan saw a need and filled it. "There wasn't any kind of school to help the really young kids," says Joan, "and yet ages two to four are children's most formative years."

She started her first program on a tiny budget in a local community center, and word of mouth soon became her most powerful ally. In two years, she had set up seven other Gymboree classes and by 1980, demand was so great that she began selling franchises. With over 200 Gymborees operating in the United States and Canada—and another 100 slated to open by the end of 1986, the continued success of Joan's venture is virtually assured.

There are other qualities usually possessed by successful entrepreneurs, and you should decide whether they are or are not part of your psychological makeup.

The desire for a personal fortune may rise very gradually to the surface of your consciousness. You may have worked for years at a satisfactory salary, with adequate prospects of promotion, but you're reaching the age when your expenses are increasing (your children may be approaching college age) and you have to think about security in the long term; or you may be a young, single woman who's decided marriage is not for you; or you may have been recently widowed. That's when many women find themselves taking out a subscription to *The Wall Street Journal* and avidly reading the success stories of new enterprises; that's when all that Horatio Alger stuff no longer seems so corny.

If you're in any of these categories, you may start comparing your own potential as an independent operator with that of other people who have made good on their own, and you may be wondering why you shouldn't get some of those goodies at the top of the money tree for yourself instead of your employer.

The desire for fame may be another motivating factor. If you're the entrepreneurial type, you may be irked by the fact that up till now, everything you've accomplished rebounds to the greater glory of a trademark or family name. (Why Eastman Kodak, Estee Lauder, Diane von Furstenberg, instead of your name?) The thrill of seeing your own name in a newspaper advertisement or on an office sign, or hearing it in a television commercial, might not be the overriding factor in your determination to start your own company. But you obviously have a healthy ego, and you'll derive a definite satisfaction from a separate and highly visible identity.

Another strong drive is the pure joy of winning. Only as entrepreneurs can we fully experience the exhilaration of outdoing the competition. The excitement of commercial combat, the delight in battling with your wits (and winning), the fierce pride in matching yourself against your rivals may provide you with more satisfaction than anything else in starting your own business. Thomas Alva Edison never demonstrated any aversion to piling up a fortune on his many inventions, but he once said: "I don't care so much about making my fortune as I do for getting ahead of the other fellows." Helena Rubinstein is candid about the intense joy she felt in over outmaneuvering and surpassing the competition.

There is one last factor to be weighed in determining whether you should join the ranks of the entrepreneurs, and that is the personal one. Such a move, you must realize, will complicate relationships. You will have less time for people close to you, less occasion for the emotional comforts offered by and to children, lovers, friends.

If you're a married woman and value your marriage, you must be assured of the wholehearted support of your mate. If you're divorced or widowed and have children emotionally or financially dependent on you, you'll have to take their needs and natures into account. People who've been through it say that being married both to a person and to a company you've founded can be one of the most demanding of experiences, taxing all your reserves. There is the price of success to be considered, as well as its rewards. But with this one as with all the other factors I've discussed, only you can make the decision.

6
Creating Your Business Plan

If you intend to establish your own business, you must have a clear blueprint far in advance. A business plan, in fact, should be the first step you take. It's vital, because it forces you to work your way through those demanding questions: Will it work? How will it work? Will I make any money at it?

Your business plan has other values beyond self-appraisal. It forms the basis for presentations to banks from whom you may need to borrow money or to firms that might invest in your business (called venture capital firms). It may also be used to persuade suppliers to grant you credit, to convince prospective customers of the viability of your enterprise and the advisability of placing orders with you. And, obviously, it can be used to attract private investors.

Whenever you make a "money presentation," for any reason, you need a business plan. Money people are naturally impressed with words and numbers—facts around which they can form a decision. It's always difficult to make a decision involving money based on oral presentation. As you read this chapter, think of your plan's wider uses—such as the next time you need a loan from your bank for an addition to your house.

Your business plan, in fact, is your key selling tool to the world until you can stand on your own financial feet, a scenario of what you hope for and believe you can accomplish — what I refer to as the "who, what, why, when and how much" plan. It should answer the tough question you'll probably be asked more than once: "What have you got to offer that can't be found elsewhere in the marketplace from an established firm?"

Basically, a formal business plan is a comprehensive document which describes a proposed new business — or a new venture for an existing business. Creating a business plan can be a costly and time-consuming task, depending on the size of the venture, the amount of capital required and the complexity of the proposed business. The main purpose of a business plan, sometimes called a feasibility study, is to provide an adequate and detailed description of the venture and, more important, sufficient evidence of the business' potential.

The well designed plan can actually play a large part in *making* the business work, in that it forces a prospective entrepreneur to organize her thoughts logically. There's a sort of magic which comes from taking out the felt-tip pen and legal pad: it pushes one from the musing, head-scratching stage to a well thought out idea. Organizing your thoughts on paper (or a computer screen) can help you determine initially whether or not the deal makes sense.

The business plan provides the lender, venture capitalist or private investor with the information needed for making an investment or credit decision. A business plan is not just a good idea, it's an *essential* step if you're trying to raise capital.

In essence, you've got to convince your reviewers that you've done your homework. Your concept may be very appealing, but without thorough preparation, your plan will fall flat on its face. In other words, you've got to do more than just describe a good marketing idea. A good plan will contain a comprehensive marketing plan including, for example, new client potential, pricing policies, and a budget and course to action for advertising and public relations. Attention to detail in a plan indicates attention to detail in business: it shows not only *what* an entrepreneur thinks but, more crucially, *how* he or she thinks.

More than just a blueprint for building a business, the plan becomes a valuable reference manual once financing has been arranged, because it outlines who will do what, and when and how it will be done.

The following outline, I feel, serves as a basic guide to what a business plan should include:

1) Summary
2) The company, and its products and services, compared to the industry as a whole
3) Market analysis and research
   — customers or clients
   — market size and trends
   — competition
   — estimated market share (and estimated sales)
   — ongoing market evaluation
4) Marketing plan
   — overall strategy
   — pricing
   — sales tactics
   — ongoing customer relations and services
   — advertising and promotion
5) Design and development
   — status and tasks
   — difficulties and/or risks
   — new and/or improved services
   — estimated costs
6) Operating/Production plans
   — geographical location
   — facilities and improvements

7) Management team
  – organization and key personnel
  – ownership and management compensation
  – supporting professional services
8) Overall schedule
9) Potential problems/critical risks
10) Financial plan
  – profit and loss forecast
  – cash flow analysis and balance sheet
  – breakeven chart
11) Proposed company offering (where outside financing is being sought)
  – desired financing
  – use of funds
  – capitalization

Of all the items listed above, your initial summary is perhaps the most important element of your plan. Make it brief (two pages or less), and concise. Your summary should provide a mini-description (covered in more detail later) of how much money is being requested, anticipated funding from other sources, and how the funds will be allotted. If collateral or ownership might be offered, say so, and list the individuals involved.

The rest of your plan should be concise as well, and easy to follow. Even if you're seeking venture capital, it's unlikely a prospective lender will review your plan from cover to cover. But you can be assured that certain parts will be scrutinized closely — and you have no way of knowing beforehand which sections those will be — so cover your bases and don't cut corners.

To provide an example, I'll quote from one business plan I put together for a proposed venture called Cortrex Corporation, for which I sought to raise $250,000 in financing. If you've never seen a business plan, it will give you a quick picture. The Cortrex plan was 14 pages long, and the table of contents read as follows:

Table of Contents

At the outset, I explained that Cortrex was designed to become a "leading producer of audio cassettes for the fields of business and finance. . . . The company plans to create, produce and distribute informational, educational, and training cassettes; and to market cassettes produced by other companies. The company projects a profitable posture by the eighth month of operation, with achievable sales increases projected for years two and three."

I then explained that the cassette field promised rapid growth, that the sales had leaped from $5 million in 1966 to an expected $200 million by 1975. To bridge the normal, non-income-producing months of initial operation, Cortrex had begun negotiations with a cassette-producing firm to distribute a number of their tapes and "allow Cortrex to realize substantial sales by the third month of operation." (It's important, obviously, to indicate to prospective financial backers that, as a young struggling company, you will have revenue coming in as quickly as possible.) I then listed a number of subjects on which Cortrex planned to produce tapes.

As you can see, the business plan anticipates the general questions outsiders are going to ask. After all, few people know your company or market the way you do. Since it's essential to prove that you know the market, and how to tap it, I then outlined our marketing plan. Cortrex would use both direct-mail campaigns and space advertising. "For the business tapes, four-part, direct-mail pieces will be sent to small and middle-sized companies."

Tie-ins with other companies to distribute Cortrex's cassette programs when they became available were also cited, with the explanation that "these companies will afford Cortrex a highly trained, professional sales force to market its products."

To provide a complete and fair picture of the field I proposed to enter, I listed leading competitors, up to and including such companies as Time-Life, with an estimated annual sales volume of $2 million in their tape division, and the Success Motivation Institute, with a $12 million estimated annual sales volume.

To indicate the source of the material to be recorded on our tapes, I reported that Cortrex would retain an author who was previously director of personnel training for a leading financial institution. . . . "Other authors have been tentatively selected but will not be approached until financing for the company has been concluded."

One of the two recording studios in the Los Angeles area would be selected to produce the master tapes. "We do not anticipate doing our own in-house tape duplication until the fourth month, at which time the volume will warrant the purchase of a cassette duplicator," I further explained. "The price difference between in-house duplication and outside duplication is approximately 20 cents per tape, or 15 percent."

This business plan was designed simply to demonstrate that I knew the field and the market I was proposing to enter and how and what to produce.

Prospective backers, of course, want to know the precise way in which the financial management of the projected company will be handled. This comes under the heading of "The Financial Plan."

I also outlined my qualifications to be chief executive officer of Cortrex, including my previous career and my experience as sales manager and a corporate officer of Infonics. I also listed an advisory board of three leading figures in the audio-visual field.

At the back of the brochure I laid out the "earnings forecast" for the first year of operation. You have to be realistic in making such a projection, since prospective backers know that a new company isn't going to take off like a rocket in its first twelve months of operation.

In my forecast I projected a gross margin (the difference between sales and cost of sales) of $102,262. Offsetting this was a total of $125,541 in selling expenses, salaries and fees, rent, phone and utilities, postage, travel, office supplies, insurance and contingencies. Thus I forecast a net loss of $23,279 for the first year of operation — modest under the circumstances, but realistic considering my intention to keep operating expenses to a minimum.

The second section of the earnings forecast reflected a more cheerful attitude, and ran as follows:

	Year Two	Year Three
Net Sales	$370,000	$585,000
Cost of Sales	144,000	222,000
Gross Margin	226,000	363,000
Selling & G&A Exp.	178,000	282,000
Net Profit Before Taxes .	48,000	81,000
Income Taxes	18,000	34,000
Net Earnings	30,000	47,000

My particular prospectus offered a positive picture, yes, but not overly optimistic considering the growth industry I was proposing to enter.

I also included a "balance sheet forecast," and a "source and application of funds forecast" for the first year of operation.

My prospectus for Cortrex wasn't the perfect model of a business plan, but it contained the essential ingredients, and could be effectively applied to many different kinds of business ventures. I bound the copies of my prospectus in good-looking black covers complete with a table of contents and page numbers. Each copy was also dated and numbered, and I kept a log detailing who had received them and when. It's not a particularly good idea to have them floating around. (In fact, the SEC has a rule to the effect that you have to file an expensive "public issue" prospectus when the number of prospective investors reaches 35.)

The quality of presentation is particularly important in a prospectus. It must, of course, be neat, clear and professionally typed and photocopied. The presentation represents you; it's your selling tool. It therefore should look as good as you and your potential investment opportunity.

In starting up your own business, even if you're not seeking large-scale financing, you should draw up a business plan — not only as a prospectus for anyone you hope to interest in the venture, but, just as important, for your own guidance and self-analysis.

7

Launching Your Own Business

Once you've decided to go on your own and begin founding a business, you'll soon learn that when successful business people say "success costs money," they aren't being simple-minded. The biggest problem the budding entrepreneur usually faces is her lack of financial expertise.

She may have a brilliant idea for a new and needed product, she may be a crack operator in the sales field, she may be a highly capable administrator, but the new company head rarely understands that the more success she hopes to achieve, the more financing she'll need. If your business takes off on a sudden upward trajectory, you'll have to find financing for a bigger inventory, more accounts receivable, an increased payroll, and perhaps larger quarters. You'll have a money crunch brought on by success rather than failure.

When Infonics' sales increased 500 percent, we were faced immediately with the problem of how to raise an amount of money substantial enough to keep pace with such rapid expansion. We had two choices: Debt financing and equity financing. Debt financing is similar to securing a loan from a bank; equity financing entails giving up part of your corporation in exchange for funding. We chose the second approach; in exchange for a healthy chunk of the company, we received over $1 million, and Infonics became a publicly held corporation. Again, the more successful you are, the more money you will need.

Recently I did some consulting with two women who told me they were talking with the Small Business Administration about a $250,000 loan. It quickly became obvious that the sum would last them only nine months. I suggested they increase their proposal by at least another $100,000 and then went on to explain why. You must plan on at least an eighteen-month period to get your new company working, whether it's a glass boutique or a motor scooter plant. It will take that long to resolve your start-up problems and become sufficiently stable.

That's why, as I've stressed earlier, it's so important to develop a sound relationship with a bank well in advance. Make yourself visible to your bank officer. Your character and your ability to convey its essence to the person who has to decide on business loans will be a crucial factor in determining whether or not you get the money to expand in step with your increased business volume.

When I was looking for a new business after selling Infonics, I surveyed the prospects of 132 companies, as well as an equal number I turned down on the phone. Many of them were faltering, or they wouldn't have been inviting outside participation. The one thing they had in common, I found, was a frightening lack of financial expertise at the top.

A problem experienced by virtually all beginning entrepreneurs is the necessity of cutting expenditures right down to absolute essentials. One firm we looked at was in debt a cool $250,000 after one year of operation, and had more than $20,000 invested in office furniture alone. It was the most beautiful potential bankruptcy in town.

Don't bedazzle yourself with the idea that a flashy front, a bold splash in the marketplace or a blast of advertising trumpets is going to clear your path like a bulldozer. Too often a person starting a business is eager to impress friends and associates and instead of putting the emphasis on the customer, spends too much money on office decor, fancy brochures and flashy ads. Until the money comes rolling in, it may be a good idea to have a low-cost outfit type your letters rather than hire an expensive secretary, or do your own decorating and cleaning. In any case, it's never a good idea to let yourself be carried away with the grandeur of your new position.

Far more important than putting up a flamboyant front is carefully balancing your income against expenses, and conserving your funds for the expensive process of searching out that market for your product or services (unless, of course, you've done the classic thing — gone into competition with your former employer — in which case you know that market as well as he does). Instead of jumping into a marketplace, I've started and ended at least three companies in the business plan stage. If you can't pull it together in a few pages, don't waste your time trying to make it work in the market. Before you go into business for yourself you should be equipped with a complete financial forecast for at least a year. If you lack financial training, get some expert assistance in this sector.

You'll find that you'll incur enough expenses without indulging in luxuries. Stationery and business cards are a must, but keep the letterhead simple and dignified. If your firm or product lends itself to an exciting trademark, colophon, or logotype, such as the famous script of General Electric or the Mercedes-Benz tricon, use one — visual impact and identification are often worth more than words. But choose one that's simple, tasteful and first quality. If you employ a graphic artist to design your logo choose someone who specializes in that type of design and ask for samples and references from satisfied clients.

You'll need the services of an outside accountant. Usually you would be well advised to choose a certified public accountant — that is, one who has passed the difficult CPA examination given by your state. Accountants range from the small one-person professional around the corner to the "Big Eight" — the largest accounting firms — the biggest of which is Peat Marwick Mitchell and Company. The fee is generally in direct proportion to the size and prestige of the accounting firm, and you will have to balance your accountant's expertise and depth of experience with what you can afford to spend on his or her services.

A word of caution: I've found that all too often accountants tend to manipulate numbers, without truly understanding their significance. It's crucial, therefore, that you attempt to judge how knowledgeable your accounting adviser really is in the meaning of numbers as opposed to their manipulation.

A decision will have to be made immediately, of course, as to what sort of legal form your business will take: a proprietorship (one-person operation), a partnership or a corporation.

Incorporating, which requires the services of an attorney, will usually cost from $700 to $1,000. The primary reason for incorporating is to avoid personal liability. For example: If a caller at your office falls over a misplaced chair and breaks his leg, he can sue the corporation but not the corporation's owner, for damages. If you take out a loan, the corporation — not you personally — is responsible, although a bank will usually make you personally guarantee the loan (this is standard bank practice in the case of small, privately held companies). If the corporation goes bankrupt, your personal assets and property can't be seized for repayment of debts. And incorporating provides another advantage over partnerships: If you have a partner and he obligates the company beyond its resources, you may have to make good for debts incurred on behalf of the partnership. The creditors will look to whichever partner has the greater ability to pay, regardless of who incurred the obligation.

One drawback to incorporating is that you have to pay

corporate income taxes as well as a personal income tax on dividends. Under certain circumstances this can be avoided under Subchapter S in the Federal Tax Code, which allows the income of a corporation to be taxed directly to the stockholders. If you do not elect the Subchapter S route, the corporation will have to pay corporate taxes on all its net income; when it declares dividends to you, its stockholder, you will then have to pay personal income tax on those dividends. This is double taxation and can readily be avoided through a Subchapter S election. Your accountant can explain it.

If you issue stock in your company, you should investigate Section 1244 of the Internal Revenue Code, which provides that, if you've taken a loss on your stock by selling it below your original cost or by having it become worthless, you can deduct up to $25,000 a year from your income. Your attorney will advise you on the rules and regulations governing the issuance of the stock, which differ from state to state and will usually take care of the legal details of incorporation.

Another question to be given serious consideration is whether you should buy a going concern rather than starting one yourself. Buying can be attractive—after all, someone else has done the groundwork. You might also seek to acquire the unprofitable division of a large company. However, this is a highly sophisticated area of finance and requires considerable capital, and its ramifications are beyond the scope of this book. Suffice it to say that there can be substantial bargains in this field, but only for those who have the expertise such a venture demands.

Be conceptually creative: Fit your prospective business venture to your own strengths. As the chief executive of such an enterprise, you should be well rounded enough to understand the sales, manufacturing, engineering, purchasing, financial, and accounting aspects of the operation. Your main strength as an entrepreneur will probably be in one of those areas, possibly two, but you've got to be able to deal with problems affecting all of them.. If you are deficient in one or more of those areas, you should seriously consider taking in a partner or partners who have the abilities you lack.

Tailoring your talents to the product or service you'll be offering is also worth serious consideration. The amount of knowledge and/or experience you'll need for supplying a product will generally be more than you'd have to demonstrate if your venture dealt in a service. Manufacturing electric motors is more complicated than running a soft-serve yogurt establishment, though even small and seemingly simple enterprises have their intricacies and pitfalls.

The main thing is to discover and acknowledge your deficiencies in advance. So many enterprises crash because of a flaw, discovered too late, in the business background of the founder. Cover your deficiencies before you start operating, because it may be too late once the wheels are turning. It's amazing how swiftly a financial shoestring can become frayed and snap.

Look for businesses within businesses. An architect who wants to branch out on her own could go into interior design, or specialize in designing convention booths, or coordinate the engineering and landscaping for a condominium complex.

A feasible scheme can often be found more or less in your own backyard. Take the case of Dorothy Sarnoff, who used her theatrical background to devise courses for people who needed training in public speaking. She recognized the need for a product to go with the service she was offering. That product was a book, *Speech Can Change Your Life*, which was not only successful in its own right but brought in as clients the people who read it. Another example is Jean Nidetch, the founder of Weight Watchers, who took advantage of the fact that she had been fat as a girl and made a career out of helping other people conquer their weight problems. Her angle was to combine dieting with the reinforcing principles of Alcoholics Anonymous. She held the first meeting of her group in her own home; eventually, with her husband and a friend brought in as a business manager, she launched her franchise system on an international basis. Having capitalized on her sales ability, plus a brilliant idea, she made a resounding success of the venture.

Should You Buy A Franchise?

Franchises can be an exciting and profitable investment vehicle; last year franchise earnings in the United States amounted to more than $500 billion. Providing you're not dealing with fly-by-night operators who take your money and leave you high and dry, buying a franchise can be a relatively painless way to start your own business.

You have to assure yourself, first of all, that the franchise offers a product or service with marketability in your community; it has to fit *local* needs. The advantage of a franchise is that you have your business charted for you, with every detail of the operation laid on—including site selection (though not always), cooperative advertising and the provision of supplies. Some highly successful franchise operations are Kentucky Fried Chicken, McDonald's® , H&R Block and Postal Instant Press (PIP).

Background and track record are extremely important if you're considering purchasing a franchise. A franchise's strongest assets are its reputation, experience, know-how and goodwill. Ask the franchisor to provide a complete rundown of the business history and success record of the franchise. If the company is publicly held, you can get that information from a prospectus or annual report. I can't emphasize too strongly the importance of obtaining a disclosure statement, which must, by law, include very specific information about the business history and financial position of the company, including past or pending litigation.

Franchise deals vary widely. Some, such as McDonalds® , include a complete business package that can't be modified. Others offer a name, a location and not much more; still others allow for varying degrees of independence. It's essential to determine in advance the precise arrangements of a franchise you're considering—whether the franchisor provides training for you and your employees, whether the franchisor provides assistance in obtaining financing, and just how nearby help is should you have a pressing question or problem.

To substantiate a franchisor's claims, ask for the names, addresses and phone numbers of at least five other franchisees. Ask them how satisfied they've been with their operation, and then ask them about revenues, franchisor support and problems.

Beware of resales of existing franchises, as the truly profitable operations are rarely resold. If an owner wants to dispose of a money-making franchise for personal reasons, chances are the franchisor will take over the business.

In the final analysis, you need to consider whether the franchise suits your particular investment personality. If you've spent your career in a quiet, detail-oriented line of work, a franchise requiring you to operate in an outgoing, high-pressure sales mode might be a mismatch.

Keeping A Lid on Operating Costs

As your business gets rolling, you should take full advantage of the fact that many people will be eager to help you on your way. You'd be amazed at how many friends a struggling young business attracts—provided you're not too proud to accept their help and don't resent what may seem at times to be a patronizing attitude.

Don't hesitate to seek advice, a commodity that many knowledgeable people are pleased to offer. A successful businessman or businesswoman can help you over many hurdles, spot defects in your method of operating, save you the trouble and pain of making your own mistakes by recalling theirs. Such a person can often widen your potential market by giving you referrals, suggesting people or companies that can use your product or service.

Suppliers are a vital source of help. If you need credit for supplies, lay it on the line. If you're completely candid with them, you'll convince them that they're taking a risk on a person of integrity. Pay their bills promptly the first time around to establish both credit and credibility. (If you can't, you should not have gone into business in the first place.) Suppliers will be eager to help you succeed. You're a customer, after all, and your success will contribute to their profits. And they, too, can provide invaluable marketing tips.

Bankers, for much the same reason, can also take a friendly interest in getting your venture off the ground. Again you must establish credibility, especially if you're operating on a shoestring. To guide a banker whose help you need, compile a pro forma statement listing your liabilities as well as your prospects for success. As I've mentioned earlier, bankers are vitally interested in the success of new ventures, despite their hard-nosed reputation. They don't spend millions of dollars on institutional advertising just to attract the finance committees of General Electric and United States Steel. Some of these very large banks have a small business investment company, known as an SBIC, whose specific purpose it is to make risk investments in small companies. Frequently these investments take the form of loans convertible into stock. There are, in addition, many SBICS not owned by banks, which may provide a source of funds for a small enterprise. Scrutinize their contracts carefully with your attorney before committing your company.

Distributors, who provide wholesale outlets for a particular industry, can also be helpful to the beginning entrepreneur, especially by coming up with pricing and marketing suggestions. They can help you avoid making disastrous mistakes in overpricing for your potential market, which will keep you in a competitive position with any rivals you may have.

Educators should not be ignored as a source of inspiration and guidance. Many professors are business consultants on the side. You may find their professional advice too expensive, but there are other advantages in keeping in touch with the faculty of the nearest university or college. There are benefits on both sides. From you they learn how technology that was developed in their studies or laboratories can be applied in your field. From them you can obtain technical and financial guidance of all kinds, often free. Don't be shy about seeking advice from the academics; true, they may sometimes seem impractical, but select what you can make best use of from their theoretical ideas, and ignore the rest.

There are details in the process of making your enterprise stand out which may seem minor but can nonetheless be very important: the design of your company's logotype, answering business correspondence promptly, overseeing the way the telephone is answered. I am not recommending pretentiousness in conceiving a corporate image; I am recommending that you put your best foot forward. Call it professionalism, if you're tired of the word "image."

If you have a worthwhile product or service to sell, you owe it to yourself to enhance it in any legitimate way that applies—packaging, merchandising, ingenuity, advertising, promotion. Otherwise you won't be able to compete successfully with rivals who may offer an inferior product or service that is merchandised well.

The aura with which you make your venture attractive to the buying public will help to clear an initial place in the market. But it's only a means to a desired end, a tactic rather than a strategy. As Robert Townsend put it, "Image is not a goal. It's a by-product. A good image has to be earned by performance." The real goal, he stresses, is "customer satisfaction, and shareholder satisfaction."

As any good coach will tell you, one invariably learns more from losing than from winning. Looking back on my own mistakes, I want to stress several points that may seem self-evident but are for that very reason often neglected.

If you're determined to start your own business, you should first try to make certain that you'll derive more profit from it (while working harder, of course, and being assailed by all the slings and arrows of your independent status) than you would from a salaried job. Profit, rather than ego gratification, should take priority. (However, the real satisfaction of entrepreneurship has its own priceless value.)

Don't try to be something you're not. If you're trained in engineering, don't insist on taking over the marketing phase of your operation. If you're not detail-oriented, make sure you associate yourself with someone who will see to it that invoices go out on time and are paid. Genius, Carlyle said, is the infinite capacity for taking pains. No matter how much drive and ingenuity you possess, you can be crippled by those little "self-evident" things.

Finally, I want to mention fear, and the fear of fear. Eden Ryl, who operates a New York training and management firm, faces this issue head on: "Failure is only temporary—never permanent—unless you let it be. Everyone is afraid of something." In the 200 motivational seminars she conducts every year, Miss Ryl emphasizes the fact that "you create your own fears, so you can eliminate them. . . . Be willing to change your attitude."

Amen to that. You must conquer fear of failing or of realizing your fullest potential by analyzing it. You'll find most of the time that the fears are only the shadows of an attitude. A negative attitude. A fear of breaking old patterns. You'll find that the world of the entrepreneur is not some trackless wilderness to be crossed—that it can be a high road to self-fulfillment.

8

Beginning Your Investment Career

Chances are, you're already an investor. Despite the fact that we're in the middle of a decade in which the "money consciousness" of most Americans has been raised significantly, most people still don't think of themselves as investors. The antiquated notion that you have to own 1,000 shares of IBM and have a "portfolio" to be termed an investor is still prevalent. The truth is, if you have an IRA, have funds in your company's retirement plan, have a savings or money market account or own your home—you're an investor. Even if all you have is a bag of silver coins, a valued ginger jar or tiffany glass, you still qualify for the title of investor.

The purpose of investing is simple: to allow your money to make more money—to put your money to work for you. Second, if you don't invest your money in some fashion or another, it's going to be eroded by inflation and cost-of-living increases. Inflation may be relatively low now, but there are no guarantees it will stay that way. Whether it rises or not, it remains a factor to be reckoned with—not only for the very rich, but especially for those in the low- and middle-income brackets.

The goal of this section of the book is to help you make the transition from casual investor to purposeful, sophisticated investor. Basic information, though helpful, is not enough. To become a competent investor, on a small or large scale, you must have what I call the "big picture." It becomes your foundation for handling the decision-making details of specific, even minor, investments.

More than anything today, the investor needs what I term an "economic weather report." To even consider investing without a solid sense of the economic scene is a bit like shooting darts. You've got to know *why* interest rates yo-yo, *why* the stock market is up versus bonds or real estate, and what the Gross National Product (GNP) has to do with you. To that end, I'll present a short course in the economics of the '80s. (For a fun and vital book on economics, pick up a copy of Leonard Silk's *Economics in Plain English*.)

For clarity on this subject, I interviewed a respected friend and expert, Bob Goodman, Senior Economist with Seligman & Co. in New York. He likens today's economy to "a steamship on a large ocean. If you're walking on the deck of that ship," Goodman says, "the ship will continue proceeding in its particular direction, regardless of the direction *you* take. Until 1979, that steamship has headed south; that year marked what I call 'the great turnaround' of the ship's wheel. The deckwalker might not have noticed the change, but the observer with an aerial view would have recognized that the ship had started heading north . . . in a positive direction."

I then asked him what he considered vital to the investor's understanding of the American economy. He replied,

> For the layperson, it's essential to understand *our* economic system—the capitalistic system. It's designed to do one thing: to produce the maximum amount of goods and services possible with existing resources, at the cheapest cost. The American economic system has served as a model for the rest

of the world for the past two centuries because, if left alone to function with its inherent *modus operandi, it works* — at least most of the time. Historically, it has outpaced and outperformed the three other systems: fascism, socialism and communism.

Despite the fact that the capitalistic system is undisputedly the finest in the world, the past 50 years have shown that it has its imperfections; and these imperfections have led to a lot of serious problems, such as inflation and recession. It became necessary, then, to impose some sort of control over the system. If the economy doesn't — or can't — run by itself, I asked Goodman, how is it controlled? He said,

Fundamentally, it is controlled by taxes and tax laws; fiscal (government spending) policies and monetary policies (the Federal Reserve Board's decisions to put more dollars into, or out of, the economy).

I then asked him how these policies have affected the economy of the '80s. He said,

As an investor, or potential investor, you need to know where we are in history. Essentially, we've reentered the producer mentality — moved away from redistribution policies — and have cut many of the government programs we simply cannot afford. Some of the decisions have been painful ones; cuts in welfare, job training and Medicare have produced hardship for many. I firmly believe, however, as do many of today's prominent economists, that "tightening the belt" has and will continue to result in a stronger, more stable economy — which in time will prove to be beneficial for all Americans, the low- and middle-income earners, as well as the rich.

Your goal as an investor, then, is to be the informed — and not the casual — observer. You needn't concern yourself with turning the system around; but it's essential that you know the direction in which it's headed, for that understanding will lay the groundwork for any and all of the investment decisions you'll make.

The Informed Investor: What Do You Need To Know?

In a recent interview with Dr. Jerry Puhlman, Senior Economist with Pacific Federal in Tacoma, WA, one of the country's leading financial institutions, I asked about the issues confronting investors in the '80s. The main reason investors need to keep abreast of the "economic weather report," he believes, is simply because we're living in an era of frequent and rapid changes; today's investor has more choices than ever before.

What can we expect for the rest of the '80s and into the '90s? Puhlman is confident that the next decade will be calmer, more predictable than the volatile '70s and early '80s; that inflation and interest rates will remain relatively low. He cautions, however, that we should not expect a "ripple-less" economy, such as we experienced in the '60s when, for four years the prime rate never moved from 5¼ percent.

The federal deficit, having attained gargantuan proportions, is a cause of concern for investors and consumers primarily because of the uncertainty it creates. According to Puhlman, the burgeoning deficit will also have an impact on economic growth in general. By virtue of its size alone, the deficit gives the government less room to make adjustments to fiscal policy; without this maneuverability, the government's ability to stabilize the economy is hindered. In the long run, Puhlman says, "This could create an upward bias in 'real' interest rates (the current interest rate minus inflation), making it more costly to buy on credit. And if the proposed changes in the tax bill are passed — limiting interest deductions and lowering marginal tax rates — it will become even more expensive to leverage."

Most economists agree that we can expect current economic trends to continue along the same lines, regardless of the outcome of the next presidential elections. The changing demographics of the country, with an aging population and "baby-boomers" becoming more conservative, will result in a continuing trend toward decreased spending levels, a more production-oriented economy and low inflation and interest rates with only cyclical variations.

Know Your Indicators

In spite of this relatively rosy long-term outlook, it's more important than ever for you, the investor, to know what to look for in the short run. Keep an eagle eye on what I call the "real" indicators: the unemployment rate, changes in monetary and fiscal policy, and events of international scope which affect the economy. Your best source is the financial section of your daily newspaper. Get into the habit of at least skimming it on a regular basis. Supplement this with reading of those leading publications I've mentioned before: *The Wall Street Journal, Business Week* and *Barron's.*

Beginning With the Basics

If you approached five friends for advice on renovating your home, they'd all have different suggestions for choice of wallpaper and tiles; one would recommend a skylight and another a bay window and breakfast nook. Chances are, though, that they'd all agree on some basics: functional, energy-saving appliances, adequate storage space and a maintenance-free floor. In other words, it's a matter of first things first.

I recommend the same approach in establishing your investing priorities. And your Number One priority is ample life insurance; it's pointless to begin investing without it. Whether you are the primary breadwinner—or share that role—life insurance is your means of protecting your family, spouse or dependents in the event of your death. The astounding reality is that most people tend to protect their replacable assets—cars, jewelry and furniture—better than the one asset that cannot be replaced: your life and ability to earn an income. Even if you're single and have no dependents, you should consider buying insurance to accumulate funds for some future objectives—such as business ventures or retirement.

Life insurance is a complex subject—and has become more so since I wrote the first version of this book. Most life insurance policies contain an insurance element *and* an investment element. Basically, however, there are two types of policies: term (or temporary) insurance, and whole life (cash value) insurance. *Term insurance*, which protects you for a specific period of time (one year, five years, etc.), usually provides the most protection for the lowest cost. The hitch is that it becomes more expensive as you grow older, and that it is really only suitable for temporary needs, such as covering a mortgage balance or remaining payments on another substantial purchase.

Cash value, or whole life, insurance provides permanent insurance for the duration of your life, in exchange for a specified annual or lump sum premium. Part of this premium is applied for insurance protection, and the other part—the investment component—creates an increasing cash value. You can borrow against the cash value of your policy, usually at a relatively low interest rate, and you don't have to repay the loan. The loan(s) are simply subtracted from the value of the policy before any death or cash surrender benefits are paid.

The question of how much, and what kind, of insurance you need obviously depends on a number of factors—your income, number of dependents and lifestyle, among others. Many employers provide life insurance to their employees at a nominal cost, and it makes sense to take advantage of this benefit. Keep in mind, however, that the death benefit for such policies rarely equals more than double the employee's annual salary, and is hardly sufficient to deep a family going for more than a few years in the event of the insured's death.

Mary Harris, a Los Angeles-based Certified Financial Planner and insurance broker for Pacific Financial Companies, says that while no specific formula applies in all cases when determining insurance needs, you can get an idea of the amount of coverage you need by considering some essentials. She suggests that you draw a T-graph and divide your needs into two parts. On the left, list your lump-sum dollar requirements, which should include an "emergency" fund (the amount needed to cover living expenses and short-term liabilities in the first few months following the insured's death), and the amount needed to pay off an existing mortgage and/or other substantial debts. On the right, determine your long-term — or income — needs. A good rule of thumb for arriving at this figure is simply to multiply the present annual income by the number of years you expect to need it (for example: ten years x $40,000 = $400,000). Add the figure on the left to the one on the right, and you should have a pretty good idea of what your needs are. The figure you arrive at may sound astronomical, but adequate life insurance can mean the difference between security and financial disaster, so it's wise to get as much coverage as you can possibly afford.

Disability insurance, though expensive, is another consideration, *especially* if you are self-employed. Believe it or not, the likelihood of suffering a short- or long-term disability at the age of 30 is five times greater than the possibility of an accidental death at the same age.

When you shop for insurance, be discriminating. Make certain the company you choose is reputable and on solid ground (the company should have an "A" rating from Bests Insurance Reports, a service that analyzes the financial statements of insurance companies). Good service is essential, so ask for references from other policyholders and ask whether there is an 800 line and how claims are handled. Before signing any documents or paying your first premium, make sure that you understand all administrative charges and costs. For instance, first-year interest rates on many whole-life policies are very attractive because of the stiff competition among insurance companies, but rates and terms in subsequent years vary widely.

The second item on your list of basics is a *savings account*. Most experts recommend that you keep an amount equivalent to four to six times your net monthly income in a liquid savings account, to provide for emergencies such as the loss of a job or unexpected medical bills.

I recommend *home ownership* as a third priority. It is one investment that retains its worth regardless of the state of the economy, and even a modest home in a good location will *always* rise in value. Despite the high inflation of the seventies, and the relatively moderate inflation rates of the past few years, real estate has continued its steady climb in value. The simple truth is that there isn't going to *be* any more land — it's a commodity of limited supply for which there will always be a demand.

And, of course, there are the income tax benefits of home ownership, most of which are likely to remain intact even after the new tax bill goes into effect.

Once you've taken care of these basics, you'll need to make some decisions about what to do with your "disposable" income. In dealing with clients who are beginning their investment careers, I always stress the wide range of options — both short- and long-term — available for these funds. What you should aim for (depending, of course, on your particular circumstances) is a careful balance of low-income, low-risk assets and some more aggressive, higher-risk holdings. The following is a diagram of the financial planning pyramid I often show at seminars. I believe it demonstrates, as graphically as possible, the comparative risks and opportunities associated with various forms of investment.

FINANCIAL PLANNING PYRAMID
OR TRIANGLE

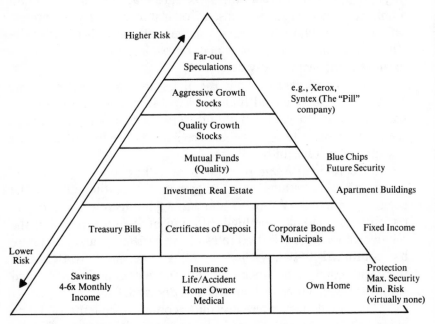

Present and Future Enjoyment

Higher Risk

Far-out Speculations

Aggressive Growth Stocks

e.g., Xerox, Syntex (The "Pill" company)

Quality Growth Stocks

Mutual Funds (Quality)

Blue Chips Future Security

Investment Real Estate

Apartment Buildings

Treasury Bills | Certificates of Deposit | Corporate Bonds Municipals

Fixed Income

Lower Risk

Savings 4-6x Monthly Income | Insurance Life/Accident Home Owner Medical | Own Home

Protection Max. Security Min. Risk (virtually none)

The purpose of this chapter is to get you started on the road to successful investing, by helping you to establish what I call "a secure base." Some of the higher-risk investments will be discussed later on in the book, so for now we'll concentrate on what I consider "super safe" investments.

Standard bank savings accounts. These pay a low rate of interest (currently about 5½ percent to 6 percent), and have a corresponding low level of risk.

Long-term (time deposit) or investment savings accounts. These accounts pay a higher rate of interest than standard savings accounts, but commit you to leaving your money on deposit for a certain period of time, usually one to four years. Penalties for early withdrawals can be substantial, so be sure you can afford to have your money tied up for the specified length of time.

U.S. Savings Bonds. Although these pay a low rate of interest, they afford a high degree of security because they are fully backed by the government. Their advantage, therefore, is primarily psychological. To obtain the full interest on these bonds, you have to hold on to them for five years. If you cash them in early, you receive very little interest, because the bulk of the interest builds up in the last years of the bond's life — so plan to keep them until they mature.

Bonds can be purchased in small denominations, starting at $100, and can be bought either through a bank or your company's payroll deduction plan.

Treasury bills. These government instruments also offer a high degree of security. They are sold in minimum amounts of $10,000, and the rate of interest is often higher than savings accounts. Treasury bill rates are set on the basis of a weekly auction, and therefore change continually, depending on the state of the economy in general. Usually, however, the rates are in rhythm with prevailing short-term interest rate levels. They mature in three, six or twelve months, and can be purchased for a nominal fee through banks or brokerage houses — or without a fee from the nearest of the thirteen Federal Reserve banks.

Government agency bonds. These bonds are issued by government institutions such as the Federal Land Bank. They pay higher rates of interest than other government issues (typically twelve percent more than U.S. Treasury bonds); they also carry a higher risk, though, since they are not direct government obligations.

Certificates of deposit. Formerly short-term IOUs issued by commercial banks, CDs are now available with maturities ranging from three months to ten years. Rates for CDs under $100,000 are fixed by the U.S. government and vary greatly depending on the term and amount of the deposit. Generally, however, they pay a higher rate of interest than regular savings accounts.

Commercial paper. Many large corporations such as General Motors and Sears frequently issue so-called commercial paper to cover their short-term financing needs. They are comparable to notes or IOUs, in which the company agrees to pay back the amount borrowed from the public in one to six months at a specified interest rate. Investing in commercial paper typically requires a minimum of $10,000 and the rate of interest usually runs about one percent higher than Treasury bills. They can be purchased through commercial banks and are backed by the credit of the issuing company, which is normally a very large, stable organization.

Money Market Funds. If investment minimums on government instruments are too high, you might look at money market funds. The best ones are invested in diversified, professionally managed portfolios of high-quality money market instruments. For most funds, the initial investment required is $2500. While the interest rates are relatively low, these funds offer current income and liquidity. They are an ideal way to earn interest on cash you expect to need in a short time, and most offer check writing privileges. You can usually buy and sell fund shares without charge, and the risk of loss of principal is minimal.

The yields from fund to fund vary somewhat, as do the privileges and requirements, so do some shopping before you invest. Most commercial banks and brokerage firms offer money market accounts.

Ginnie Maes. The nickname for the Government National Mortgage Association (GNMA), this government-owned corporation purchases mortgages from private lenders, such as banks and savings and loans, packages them into securities and sells the certificates to investors. The government guarantees regular payment of principal and interest to Ginnie Mae holders. The enormous growth of the secondary mortgage market has resulted from the efforts of Ginnie Mae, as well as two other agencies—Freddie Mac

(Federal Home Loan Mortgage Corporation) and Fanny Mae (Federal National Mortgage Association).

These agencies have greatly increased the amount of money available for home mortgages, while providing a low-risk, high-yielding investment alternative for the conservative investor. Certificates can be purchased in amounts of $5,000 and up, and can be bought through brokerage houses and banks.

Zero-Coupon bonds. These relatively new securities provide maximum safety because they're backed by the U.S. Government) and have the bonus of a compounding yield. They make no regular interest payments, but are sold at substantial discounts from their face value at maturity. When the bond matures, you collect the principal and all the accrued interest. For example, a $1000, 15-year bond paying ten percent compounded annually would be worth about $4300 at maturity.

TIGRs, short for Treasury Investment Growth Receipts, are one of the new breed of zero coupons. These, along with other variations on the theme (Stripes and CATS), represent ownership of future principal and interest payments on U.S. Treasury bonds, and therefore offer safe, predictable growth. They are best suited for long-term goals, such as funding a child's education or meeting retirement income needs. Market value on these bonds fluctuates sharply, and although the interest isn't paid until maturity, it is taxable in the year it is earned. Some types of zeros earn tax-exempt interest (municipal bonds, for instance). They can be bought in denominations of $1000 and up, and maturities range from five to 20 years.

IRA, KEOGHs, 401Ks and Other Tax Planning Investments

Your main goal in investing is to make your money make more money. A secondary goal is to keep as much of what you earn as possible, by paying the IRS only as much as you have to. Even if you're not in a high-income bracket, you should take advantage of the various tax-saving strategies for your income.

The *Individual Retirement Account (IRA)*, an innovation of the '80s, has had a significant impact on the world of personal finance. It has made savers out of spenders and turned some conservative savers into investors, with the many options available.

Just about anyone can open an IRA account, even divorcees whose only income is alimony payments, thereby sheltering at least $2000 from income taxes. An estimated 40 million Americans have opened IRA accounts, and the value of these assets has risen from $26 billion in 1981 to $170 billion in 1986.

One of the most common misconceptions about IRAs is that they're simply retirement accounts, to be opened at your local bank or through your employer. An IRA is actually an investment, and should be treated as such; your objective in opening one should be to seek the best return possible for your $2000. You can place your IRA in mutual funds, zero-coupon bonds, or CDs—in virtually any investment that qualifies as an IRA trustee.

It pays, then, to do some diligent shopping before you invest your IRA money. Of course, some of the higher yielding options carry with them a higher risk, but in the long run, an IRA investment in a moderate-risk vehicle can produce substantially higher returns.

Another consideration in IRA investing, often overlooked, is the benefit of what I call "early" or periodic funding. If you can spare the dollars, begin funding your IRA as early in the year as possible—preferably in monthly installments; early contributions will increase the value of your investment dramatically. For example, over 30 years, $2000 invested at the beginning (rather than at the end) of the year, will increase the worth of your account at retirement by $35,000!

In recent years, IRAs have been touted as the best shelter since the collapsible tent. For the most part, it's true. But depending on where you work—and whether you're self-employed—you may be eligible for other types of savings plans that can complement—or even out-perform—the IRA as an investment.

If your employer has a *401(k) plan* (named after the tax-code amendment that created it), take advantage of it. An estimated half a million U.S. employers now offer such plans to around 20 million employees. In a 401(k), your employer transfers a percentage of your gross salary, usually about ten percent, into an investment fund. Most funds invest in moderate-risk stocks or bonds, mutual or money-market funds, or interest-bearing accounts. Most plans are self-directed (you choose where your money goes) and the contributions, as with IRAs, are made with pre-tax dollars and grow tax-free until the funds are withdrawn.

The bonus of these plans is that, in many cases, employers generally match from 25 percent to 100 percent of the amount you invest in the plan. Should you retire or leave the company, you can remove the lump sum—but you'll have to be prepared for the tax consequences. A financial advisor can explain options for "rolling over" the amount or "forward averaging" to minimize the tax bite. Another plus, not allowed with an IRA, is that you can make penalty-free withdrawals from the plan if your personal dilemma falls under the employer's definition of financial hardship.

Note: 401(k) plans will probably be affected by the upcoming tax bill, but as expected changes will be phased in over a number of years, you'd be well advised to invest in one while the tax advantages are still intact.

If you're self-employed, own a business or simply have some amount of free-lance income, you ought to set up a *Keogh* plan. Like IRAs, a Keogh allows you to direct retirement assets into just about anything but collectibles. You can put away—and deduct on your tax return—up to 20 percent of your self-employment income, or $30,000, whichever is less.

You can establish your Keogh plan yourself, but the paperwork and administration involved can be quite complicated.

Your best bet is to consult an accountant before you get started. It's a first-rate tax shelter, though, and well worth the effort; it also appears that it won't be affected by the new tax bill, so it should satisfy many of your long-term objectives.

In tandem with the virtual revolution in life insurance, has evolved a breed of investments with such a range of variety and options that they have appeal for almost any investor. *Annuities*, which are essentially savings accounts sponsored by life insurance companies, are sold by brokers, insurance agents and financial planners. Like bank Certificates of Deposit, an account can be opened with a minimal deposit – and you make additional contributions, of as little as $25, as often as you wish. The insurer, in return, guarantees a specified rate of interest on your money, usually for one year.

Annuities can be styled to meet short- and long-term investment objectives, and the tax advantages are such that annuities are a viable alternative for investors in almost any tax bracket. The two types of annuities – fixed and variable – have a common trait: high fees. These vary somewhat, with some firms charging a whopping nine percent sales fee at the outset; others may charge a lower initial fee, but may impose high "surrender" charges, should you decide to take out more than ten percent of your assets in a given year.

With fixed annuities, the insurance company itself guarantees your principal. It's important, then, to deal only with reputable, major insurers – ones rated A + by Best's Insurance Reports.

Variable annuities are actually mutual funds managed by the insurer. The initial investment required is usually somewhat lower than with fixed annuities (generally $500 to $1000), though some companies offer annuities with even lower initial amounts. In a variable annuity, the life insurance company makes periodic distributions to the investor. These payments vary based on the performance of the equity securities (stocks, bonds, money markets) of the chosen portfolio.

When you decide to withdraw money from your annuity, you have two options: to take it out as a lump sum, and spend or reinvest as you wish, or to annuitize (receive monthly payments for the rest of your life). With a lump-sum withdrawal, you'll have to suffer the income-tax consequences, and pay surrender or early-withdrawal charges, if applicable. If you choose to annuitize, the amount of monthly income will depend on your age, sex and the company and pay-out option you've selected. Choosing among those options can be extremely complicated, so it's best to consult with an advisor before you sign on the proverbial dotted line, especially if your annuity represents a substantial investment or has been earmarked for retirement income.

Help in Deciding – Should You Go It Alone Or Get An Advisor?

Many of my clients, savvy and novice alike, often ask me the same question: Why should I pay fees and commissions to a broker or planner, when I can make the investment myself? There simply is no easy answer. You *can* do it yourself, and you may end up achieving as good a track record in your investing as any advisor. The point is, though, that you have to be willing, and able, to spend the time and do the research required to make sound investment choices. And that, my friends, is no small task.

The primary prerequisite for "do-it-yourself" investors, I believe, is a high and unflagging degree of interest. And that entails regular reading of such publications as *The Wall Street Journal, Barron's, Forbes* and *Business Week*. In essence, you've got to be committed to do what you're unwilling to pay the experts to do: conduct diligent research, keep up with trends, government policy, interest rates and, of course, the Dow Jones performance.

If that's not your bag, or if, like many career-track professionals, you feel your energy is better expended in doing what you do best, then by all means seek a competent advisor. Depending on your objectives, the amount of money you have to invest and what I call your "risk quotient," you can find an advisor to suit your needs.

Certified Financial Planners are a relatively new genre of financial advisors. Trained to some extent in all areas of tax and investment planning, financial planners specialize in what I call "the overall approach" to managing your finances. Most are affiliated with brokerage houses and insurance firms, and are able to implement policies and stock transactions or purchases without bringing in a third party.

Unfortunately, there is no single standard of compensation for financial planners. Some charge a flat fee for a comprehensive financial plan, which normally includes a diagnosis of a client's present situation and recommendations for tax and investment strategies to increase net worth. Others charge a percentage of the package or a combination of fee and percentage. Many planners charge by the hour, with rates varying from $50 to about $125 an hour. The rate is usually determined by the planner's experience, the size and prestige of the firm and the planner's credentials (whether he or she is a licensed securities dealer or insurance broker, etc.).

Most reputable financial planners are more than willing to work with any other advisors you have retained, such as your attorney or accountant. The introductory session with a professional planner is usually offered free of charge and gives you an opportunity to get answers to pressing questions, as well as the chance to feel out whether the planner is someone with whom you'd feel comfortable.

Although financial planners are listed in the Yellow Pages, your first choice should always be a referral. Barring that route, you can get a referral from the International Association of Financial Planners, which has more than 100 chapters across the United States. A list of Certified Financial Planners, who've received that designation by virtue of having completed a rigorous two-year

training course in addition to having a requisite amount of experience in finance-related fields, can be obtained from the Institute of
Certified Financial Planners, based in Denver, CO. Although
membership in one of these organizations doesn't guarantee
performance or ability, it does indicate a degree of commitment to
the profession. Beware of so-called planners who are employed by
a particular company offering only one product or service;
obviously their interest is going to be in selling as much of the
product as possible to earn a larger commission.

Certified Public Accountants, who specialize in income tax
planning, charge by the hour. Again, rates vary with level of
experience and size of prestige of the firm, but most accountants
charge between $50 and $150 an hour. As I mentioned earlier, the
best way to choose an advisor is to get a referral from a satisfied
client. Keep in mind, though, that most accountants tend to have
sub-specialties, i.e., corporate or small business tax planning or
personal portfolio experience. It's always important to get the best
advice you can afford, but if your needs are fairly simple, it makes
no sense to retain an accountant from one of the "Big Eight"
firms. They simply won't have the interest in a client of moderate
means, and they've got bigger fish to fry.

Registered Investment Advisors deal almost exclusively with
stock, bond and mutual fund investments. They charge by the hour
for their services and tend to have a specific bent or forte,
promoting either conservative, low-risk investment strategies or
more volatile high-risk investments.

Whether you choose a financial planner, accountant, broker
or registered investment advisor will depend on your circumstances, objectives and needs. The main issue here—even if you
decide to go it alone—is to *get started now*. Commit yourself to
beginning your investment program, even if at first it is on a very
small scale. You'll find, as many of my clients have, that there's a
positive and pervasive feeling that comes from having made the
decision to improve your future lot in life. And once you begin to

experience successes in your investing, your commitment to the ultimate goal—making your money work for you—will be a constant source of satisfaction and excitement.

9
Choosing the Pros

"If you're so smart, why aren't you rich?" It's a common question, indicative of a common dilemma: the doctor, business executive gets to the top of his or her field but flunks the test when it comes to managing personal finances.

The point is, whether you're working with a little nest egg or a potential Fort Knox, professional management of your money is critical. The main reason to have advisors is that the economy of the '80s is incredibly complex; and the tax implications, regardless of how much money you make and in spite of current or anticipated tax reform, are enormous for all of us. Even filling out a tax return has become such a complicated ordeal that it can no longer be managed by the average taxpayer.

A story I heard recently serves as an appalling reminder of the far-reaching and frightening consequences of poor money management. A prominent Southern California attorney, let's call him Michael Thomas, had been making in excess of $500,000 a year for the past five years. Yet, in 1983, he had absolutely nothing to show for the cool $2.5 million he had earned since 1978, except for a personal residence valued at $350,000, on which he still had a ten-year mortgage. His attitude about his money had obviously carried over to his wife and children who, having adopted his "spend now" philosophy, had amassed an astounding $57,000 in charge-card debt alone! He'd made a few investments over the years, but his choices had been based on bar-room conversations with enamored risk-taking colleagues, and few had panned out. Michael's liability to the IRS alone over those five years amounted to more money than many people make in a lifetime . . . a sum which could have been substantially decreased had he chosen to hire professionals early on to help him manage his money.

Michael's story had a happy ending. In 1983, he took a hard look at his finances, admitted that his expertise lay in law and not money management, and hired the best money manager he could find. Three years later, after modifying his spending habits and making prudent long- and short-term investments, Michael is doing what he should have done years ago — putting his money to work for him, with the help of competent professionals.

Michael's scenario is an extreme one, but the thinking that put him in that perilous position is shockingly prevalent. Many hard working, high-income individuals use the excuse that they're "too busy" to bother with hiring professionals. Still others are afraid to admit that they haven't the faintest idea how to go about choosing pros.

Early on in my career, people were always talking about contacting their brokers or "getting in touch with" their attorneys. Everyone seemed to have a smoothly functioning team that could be summoned forth like that amazingly helpful *djinn* in *Arabian Nights*, simply by picking up the phone. I suddenly realized that while people were always talking about accountants, brokers and lawyers, no one ever discussed how you go about getting one.

Times have changed; the atmosphere of apprehension and intimidation that surrounded selecting professionals no longer prevails. Competition is stiff, even in the upper echelons, and no well-meaning, competent professional would be inclined to turn away a potential client by barraging you with incomprehensible jargon, or making you feel that there's the whole Indian Ocean between you and the leather chair behind some massive mahogany desk.

There's simply no point in feeling that you're at a disadvantage because the pro knows something you don't — that's why you're there! Try looking at it this way: Instead of furniture, cars or clothing, a professional has special knowledge for sale, and you are deciding whether you'll hire that knowledge or not. When it comes to your finances, it doesn't pay to adopt a "jack-of-all-trades" attitude about your capabilities, especially if you're busy developing your career or business. The name of the game is getting the very best talent you can, within the framework of your needs and your budget — and reputation is of crucial importance.

I've already stressed the tremendous importance of your bankers in your campaign for financial self-realization (and no one is more vital to you), and further on I'll deal with the selection of a stockbroker. Right now I want to talk about the pattern of expertise you will need in order to achieve your financial self-realization.

In my own financial affairs, which include both business and personal needs, I've retained what I refer to as my basic seven — the pros I work with on a continual basis.

1. Banker
2. CPA/Tax Accountant
3. Lawyer
4. Insurance Agent
5. Stock Broker
6. Real Estate Broker
7. Financial Planner

You should make up your own list. You may have a need for highly specialized talents such as those furnished by an art or antiques appraiser, a business manager or patent attorney. If you do, add them to the above.

In the past ten years, a new breed of money managers have emerged — financial planners. In an era of increasing specialization among professionals, financial planners — or "money coordinators" — are a digression from the norm. Their *raison d'etre*, so to speak, is to provide overall comprehensive advice on managing your finances — covering everything from tax and investment planning to pension fund and estate planning. A professional planner should be willing to work with your other professionals — attorney, insurance agent, accountant — or whomever you're currently retaining. Their fees can be as low a $50 for a "financial plan," or as high as $7500, depending on the planner's expertise and the complexity of your financial situation. As in choosing any professional, look for professional designations. Ask whether he or she is a Certified Financial Planner (CFP), or a member of the International Association of Financial Planners. Members of these two organizations have met certain criteria, in terms of continuing education and length of experience, and should have a solid background in most areas associated with personal finance.

So how do you select those top-flight professionals for your fiscal team, the best you can afford — a team you can work with closely and effectively to achieve your goals? Over the years I've put together a simple step-by-step checklist I've found to be consistently successful in choosing all professionals, both in and outside of the financial community. Here it is:

1. Define your need. This sounds silly, but invariably you'll find it helps in clarifying and focusing your problem. Perhaps the greatest margin for error lies in asking the wrong pro about the wrong thing. Take lawyers, who many people think are automatically financial wizards. Most of them are not. Patent law and criminal law, for instance, are like apples and bananas and have no tie-in with finance. I remember a friend talking about a real estate

negotiation and saying of her legal counsel, "But he was only a corporate lawyer, he didn't know enough about real estate to be very helpful." In other words, she should have consulted a real estate lawyer. Today there are specialists within the specialty. We live in a diversified, highly technical world. Recognize that.

The single exception here is, of course, the attorney who specializes in areas of the financial field such as taxation or estate planning. By defining your need you may also find you can get your answer or have your matter handled without fee by your banker, say, or by your employer or even yourself (with a little vigorous research at the local library)—in which case you'll save yourself some money. You also should determine how long you'll be needing these services, whether on a one-shot or an ongoing basis.

2. Make a list of three. Once you've ascertained that you require, for example, an attorney, get the names of three—not less, and probably not more. (I've found that more than three involves too much time and effort.) Here are ways to find that list:

a) Ask your friends or family members for referrals. Provided you're seeking the same type of assistance, a satisfied client will be your best source of referrals.

b) Use the company where you work, or that of a friend. It will have at least one legal counsel.

c) Use reference books. (I'll go into this a bit further on.)

d) Contact an organization representing professionals in your particular field of inquiry. There are associations of lawyers, accountants, financial planners, etc. You can find these associations by consulting the Yellow Pages or the library's list of associations.

e) Ask your banker.

Early in my working career, it took me much too long to realize that I was sitting within 50 feet of an upturned cornucopia of resources. The first time I used my company as a source of guidance was in getting a car loan. My boss enthusiastically suggested that I talk with the firm's banker, which started the machinery. You've never in your life seen such incredible personal service over a matter as basic as a car loan.

Two qualifications for accepting any recommendations, corporate or otherwise, are (1) that you respect the source of the reference and (2) that you make sure your good Samaritans understand that it's *only* a reference — the final choice is yours, and some people get really possessive over giving references. For instance, you might want to say: "I'm in the market for a good tax attorney. Do you know one I should interview?" Also, I never take a reference's quality for granted. Everyone has a unique personality and a particular problem. Also, of course, the person whose help you're seeking may very well not know all there is to know about the referent's abilities.

3. Secure a face-to-face interview. This is the most crucial of the four steps. Understanding the purpose of the interview is all-important. Be perfectly clear in your mind about this. You are not seeking favors or begging assistance or otherwise improperly taking the Great One's time. You are hiring a professional — buying his or her specialized skill — to assist you in achieving your desired goal.

I particularly enjoy the interview approach because it enables me to gather all the information I need in an upbeat fashion, sitting across the desk from someone. (If you do decide to use this person, the two of you will be working together in just this way or on the phone, so the personal interview is in a sense a preview of what your relationship will be like.) After you've made up your list of three, call for appointments several days in advance. Be sure you raise the question of a fee in this initial telephone call. Should there be a fee for this brief preliminary meeting, make up your mind at this point whether or not you're willing to pay it. I would not be inclined to pay one, since most reputable firms (including legal firms) do not charge for a bona fide introductory meeting.

A word of caution here: Some very busy people may want to handle this question-and-answer session on the phone. Don't acquiesce. Press, however pleasantly, for a face-to-face meeting and don't be put off. Depending on the complexity of your problem or situation, the interview should take about fifteen minutes. Be prepared yourself and don't waste the professional's time—or your own. Remember, this is only an interview; your decision will come after you've seen all three of your candidates and gathered all the relevant information.

In an interview like this I use the following list of queries. (For special or unusual meetings I add pertinent questions or comments to it.) The seven points you want to be sure to cover are these:

- How old is the firm or institution?
- How many people are in the firm?
- In what areas do they specialize?
- What is the background of the person with whom you're talking? This would include schooling, degree, experience and so on, and position with the firm.
- Who are his or her other customers or clients? If he can't or won't provide names, at least try to find out what their profiles are like: companies or individuals, prominent or obscure, complex or simple.
- What are the precise fees or percentages involved?
- Does he or she have direct experience in your area of need?

Bear this in mind: The interview actually begins the moment you enter the offices. Surroundings often reflect the nature or capabilities of the occupant, so don't discount a questionable or disconcerting environment. Little things can sometimes tell you more than big things. Does the support staff look capable? Are their desks in what a broker friend of mine calls "efficient disorder"? (I, for one, have never bought the propaganda about "a sterile desk equaling a fertile mind.") You want to feel good about a firm with which you're sharing your future. Pay attention to the vibes. Even the decor can be revealing. Don't fall for phony opulence.

Pay particular attention to the opening moments of your interview with your professional. This is when most people reveal their attitudes most clearly. A well-recommended accountant once kept a friend of mine cooling her heels in his outer office for over an hour, offered the most casual of apologies for this inconvenience, and then called in one of his secretaries and began giving her lengthy instructions on correspondence concerning other clients.

"I don't care how good they said he was," my friend told me. "Anybody that rude and that disorganized isn't going to be reliable enough to handle my tax problems."

Nevertheless, be realistic. You may encounter someone who's simply too big to want to work with you. If a top real estate broker works primarily in the $350,000 property market and your interest lies in $90,000 houses, a marriage probably won't be to the advantage of either of you. Don't take offense at this, or try to fight an already accomplished fact, hoping they'll change firm policy just for you. You can't afford such self-indulgence. Be sure to explain clearly and concisely your interest or situation at the outset, and then listen for their response. (Your explanation should cover who, what, where, how and why.)

At this point, you can expect your referent to start selling. All people in the professional categories I've listed wear sales hats, too—they're in the service business, remember. The "sell" may be very direct, involving an analysis of situations similar to yours that the firm has solved effectively; or it may be very subtle—a discernible warmth of manner and a remark such as "I really look forward to hearing from you again about this."

These are the nuances you should weigh. Watch for attitude—alertness, clarity of expression and, most of all, genuine interest in your problem. People run businesses, and human nature is the mainspring of the financial world just as in any other.

Some years ago I interviewed a lawyer who suddenly broke off early in our interview to apologize for being in his shirt sleeves and without a tie and then launched into a long, involved discourse on how he came to hate jackets and ties during army duty in New Guinea during World War II. This digression told me several things about him: He lacked the impersonal austerity you need in a lawyer. He had suddenly started thinking of me personally, and not as a client with a rather complex problem that needed solving. Also, he was indecisive: If not wearing a jacket and tie embarrassed him, he should have put one on before the meeting, or he should have sat there tieless and not indulged in any apologies. Furthermore, he lacked discipline. He knew I had claims on my time as he did on his, but he chose to wander off down memory lane. And finally, he was dangerously self-centered: I had no interest at that moment in listening to his tales of the South Pacific, fascinating though they might have been, but I was offended that his affairs interested him more than a prospective client's. These qualities simply do not combine to make the mixture you seek in legal counsel. Needless to say, I crossed him off my mental list and concluded our interview.

Trust your instincts. If, after careful observation, a person rubs you the wrong way, my advice is to keep looking. There are plenty of other professionals out there; chances are you'll find someone with whom you can work harmoniously. But don't be taken in by charm alone, either. It's a professional you want, not an escort or a friend.

Don't make a snap decision during the interview. Stick with your game plan. You may feel that a particular person or firm is the answer to your professional prayers; but in most cases you should give yourself time to make a dispassionate decision. A good exit line that doesn't imply any commitment on your part is: "If it should turn out that we'll be working together on this, what would the procedure be?" Accent the should if you like. You have left the situation open; now you are free to return home or to your office, make a comparison with the other two people you've interviewed, and come to your decision at your leisure.

A few minor points: If you feel uncomfortable at first about doing the interview alone, you may prefer to take someone along — who, by the way, should be fully briefed on your ground rules. You may present your companion as an assistant or business associate, if you like, to explain his or her presence. Two heads are frequently better than one (depending on the person and the situation, of course!), even if only one is doing the talking. Don't be afraid to jot down the professional's responses to your queries. If he takes offense at this, you don't want to retain him anyway, and this way you'll have notes to refer to when making your final decision. You may also want to use three-by-five file cards to check off your questions as you go along, though it's better to commit your basic seven points to memory. It frees you for other thoughts and observations.

4. Decision for action. This is your final step. Take your time, weigh the various attributes of your three candidates — expertise, personal interest, background, qualifications for your particular problem or enterprise — and make your decision. Make sure that you know exactly how you are going to proceed: the costs, time involved and a firm idea of when you can expect to attain your anticipated objective. Don't be embarrassed about putting it in writing, or asking your professional to do so.

A final note: The professional who will handle some of the most complex — and crucial — issues in your life will be your attorney. In selecting an attorney, the best source, aside from referrals, is probably the Martindale-Hubbell directory. It lists most lawyers in the United States and offers a comprehensive breakdown of the personnel in each firm, their areas of specialization, and how long they've been with the law firm. Most libraries carry this directory. It is vitally important to match your need to the capability of the lawyer or firm. The advantage here is that while you should check with three references, a firm that specializes (or has a department that specializes) in, say, estate planning, may in fact be able to save you a great deal of money simply because it won't have to refer everything to its research department.

Remember, it's you who are doing the hiring, and you don't have to commit yourself until you feel you've found the right fit—a pro you like and trust. At the close of an interview, tell the professional you'll get back to him or her once you've reached a decision, and then do so. You don't have to be embarrassed to admit that you've settled on someone else, but use diplomacy in giving your reasons. Here are some I've given:

- Your fee doesn't fit within my budget.
- I'd prefer to work with someone closer to my home.
- I feel I could probably work better with someone else.

What To Expect from A Pro

At the very least, you can reasonably expect promptness and courtesy; most important, you should expect competence. Promptness means that the work gets done on time (unless there's a good, bonafide reason for a delay), and that your calls are returned within 48 hours. Courtesy entails addressing you as an equal and answering your questions (however rudimentary!) in plain English rather than jargon, re-explaining if necessary until you understand the answers.

Competence is often more difficult to judge. The longer you deal with someone, the more you'll know about his or her capabilities. We're all human, and even the most efficient pros make mistakes, but whoppers shouldn't be forgiven: The attorney who files your case in the wrong court, a realtor who continues to show you property you can't afford, or the broker who trades you in and out of stocks just to earn extra commissions.

Letting someone go is never easy. But if your advisor is incompetent, patronizing or untrustworthy—or fails to provide the services for which you're paying—you need to protect yourself. Be firm, businesslike and brief. Avoid attacking him or her personally and, above all, don't lose your temper; you'll probably regret it in the long run.

If you move through these points diligently, you will have made the best possible decision for yourself. And the pros you retain will know they too are working for a professional. You.

10

Your Safari into the Investment Jungle

Wall Street. Just the words conjure up a host of images. Fast money, big money financial feast or famine; hot-blooded traders in grey suits with ties askew, wading through wads of ticker tape on "the floor," barking orders in some incomprehensible language in the rapid-fire manner of a country auctioneer. For the unwary, Wall Street — and the stock market itself — *is* a jungle, a place to tread lightly with your senses piqued. But it's not so different from any other marketplace where the stakes are high and, unlike the gambling casinos of Las Vegas, its madness is tempered by the strict laws and regulations that govern it.

Just as the economy plays a vital role in your life and financial well-being, as an investor — or potential investor — you should be aware that the stock market business is *your* business. The market has been called the backbone of the American free enterprise system; it boasts more than 50 million investors and more than half of them are women. The market is popular, vital and exciting because it provides the opportunity to bet on the success of American business. It's other special appeal is that all investments are liquid — at any given time, there is usually a market for the purchase or sale of your investment. Market proponents often advance this argument when comparing the market to, say, real estate, which is not nearly so negotiable a security.

The more you learn about the market, the less forbidding and mysterious it becomes. In essence, learning about the market requires the same process—and abilities—as any other field of study: information gathering, diligent analysis and an acquired knack for making practical and objective decisions based on the expertise you've gained.

If possible you should take a personal look at the way Wall Street, or your nearest stock exchange, operates. Some years ago, when I first became interested in the possibilities offered by the financial world, I trekked down to lower Manhattan, made the grand tour of the New York Stock Exchange, and watched the trading activities. It's reassuring to find that the atmosphere is sober, efficient, and businesslike.

It is absolutely vital to scout the territory, study your chosen investment area, and test its feasibility with every means available to you. This doesn't exclude the exercise of good old-fashioned common sense. Shirley Chilton once told me a story that makes this point vividly:

"I'll always remember back in 1956, after I'd been promoted from the switchboard to operations manager and had become a registered representative of this company, how a little old lady kept coming in almost every day, sat near my desk, and kept watching the tape on new York Stock Exchange transactions. She was about eighty years old.

"One day she spoke up. 'Honey,' she told me, 'I want to buy a stock.' I told her I thought it would be important to be sure she had enough money in a bank account and adequate assets before she embarked upon a risk venture.

"But she said, 'I'm eighty years old, honey. I've been around. I know what I want, and I want to buy Brunswick.'

"Brunswick was a speculative issue, a company that manufactured sporting equipment and built bowling alleys, selling at about seven dollars per share. 'Don't you want to buy something more stable that pays a dividend?' I asked her. She insisted on Brunswick. So I questioned her about her financial situation to determine if she could risk investing in the stock market, decided that she could afford the risk, and had her sign a statement absolving Reeves if her hunch or whatever it was, turned out disastrously. She said she wanted to buy five hundred shares of Brunswick.

"I asked her why she picked Brunswick, and she told me, 'I often visit the bowling alley with my son. I see an awful lot of people patronizing that place. It's busy day and night, and I can't find a place to sit down. It must be a good growth business, bowling alleys.'

"Now that was a very sensible observation. The bowling alley boom had just begun. Brunswick stock went up and up. When it reached sixty-three, finally she instructed me to sell it. Again I asked her why she decided that now's the time—the stock was still on the rise. 'Because,' she said, 'when I go to the bowling alley now, I can find a place to sit down.'

"The Brunswick stock did rise higher, about ten points, after she sold it. But she had been wise in making her move when she did. The only time to sell stock is too soon. That little old lady's success in financial management is something I've never forgotten. It showed me that a woman with common sense and powers of observation can do as well as anyone else even without long-term expertise."

With a sound and sensible approach, you can find it an adventure to operate in your own personal sector of the financial world.

Of course, you don't actually have to go out and buy a stock. You can practice by selecting one from the financial pages of your newspaper, and then follow its progress on a day-to-day basis as though you owned it. That way you can, in effect, go through all the decision-making process and develop a feeling about a stock, watching all news breaks that arise with respect to that particular company—its personnel changes, its expansion, its quarterly earnings reports. While this does not hold the same emotional overtones as actual buying and selling, it's one way (especially for the more cautious) of gaining an educational base in the market.

Let's take a quick look at the Street, as it's called, and how it came about. The American stock market is almost as old as the republic, dating back to congressional authority for an $80 million bond issue to pay part of the costs of the Revolution. Some years later, in 1792, 24 bigwigs stood under a buttonwood tree on Wall Street and signed an agreement for trading stocks; this was the seedling of the New York Stock Exchange, often called the "Big Board." In the middle of the nineteenth century another outdoor market sprang up, called the Curb (that's where its members conducted their business); it later became the American Stock Exchange.

Those first two exchanges—to be followed by more than a dozen others, from Boston to San Francisco—transformed the nature of American finance and industry. Formerly, American businesses and industries had been entirely controlled by the men who invested their private fortunes in them. More and more companies, needing capital to expand with the times, began offering shares of their stock to the public to finance new growth. That's how the American economy came to be owned by millions of people, instead of remaining a tight little oligarchy.

The people who conduct the business of those exchanges, managing the sale and transfer of all those thousands of stocks and hundreds of millions of dollars, are the brokers who buy "seats" on the exchange which cost a small fortune. In addition to the New York and American Stock Exchanges, and those in various other cities, there is the over-the-counter market, which deals in thousands of minor issues—which are for the most part companies which haven't attained the size and profitability to be listed on a major exchange. The name comes from the fact that such issues were once literally traded over the counter of a bank or similar institution. Obviously stocks sold on the OTC market generally represent small companies with an uncertain future; if the companies trading over the counter succeed and grow and can meet the requirements of an exchange, they advance to the American and then to the Big Board. I'll have more to say on this later.

If you've educated yourself in the mechanics of the money game and calculated how much money you want to invest, you'll want to know how to enter the marketplace. Obviously you can't dash onto the trading floor of a stock exchange waving a sheaf of currency; that's the prerogative of the professional traders.

So you'll need an intermediary — a stockbroker.

Picking the right broker is an important part of your investment decision-making. A broker who takes an intelligent interest in your financial situation, who will further the process of educating you in the ways of the money world, will make all the difference between a good return on your money and mediocre results.

In finding a broker, you should go about the selection process very carefully. Look on it as a kind of marriage. You don't want to get stuck with the wrong kind of partner. If you don't have much money to invest, you may want to select a large firm with many local branch offices geared to the smaller investor, such as Merrill Lynch, E.F. Hutton, Shearson/Lehman, American Express, Paine Webber, or Bache and Company. But the most important key is the type and size of account your individual broker is handling.

One way to find a suitable broker is to ask your friends for someone who has proved satisfactory to them. But don't necessarily take their advice. Go around and talk to the managers of brokerages.

Your prospective broker should ask you pertinent questions to make sure you're in a position to invest in stocks. But you should do most of the questioning. Ask such questions as "What percentage of your clients have made a profit?" and "Would you please give me the names and telephone numbers of four clients who have made money with you and four who have not?" Very few people use this interview technique in selecting a brokerage to handle their investments, but they should.

Before committing yourself to any particular brokerage, it's an excellent idea to get the feel of its operations. A brokerage is partly a public place; a mirror image, in a sense, of the stock market itself. There's a large area with comfortable seats for people who simply want to come in and watch the action on an electronic board that reports the current activity on the major exchanges, the minute-to-minute fluctuations in stock prices. From sensing the atmosphere of the place and from the conversation of people around you (who presumably are clients of the firm), you'll gather an impression of the way it operates. Many of the larger establishments have information officers whose responsibility it is to answer any questions you may have.

The broker probably will also explain to you the dividend factor. Stocks paying high dividends are not usually growth issues, but are fine for long-term investment because they provide you with a steady income.

Choosing Stocks: Know Thyself, Know the Market

Once you've found a broker you feel you'd like to work with, you need to get a clear picture of just how much you want to invest and what kind of stocks you want to buy (blue chips, glamour issues, growth stocks or high-risk/venture capital issues).

Regardless of your choice, the most critical factor to consider is *timing*. The only time to invest in the stock market is when it's positive — which means that over 50 million shares are being traded daily. The big players in the market are the pension funds — Teamsters, General Motors, Chrysler Corporation,

Teachers — and a host of other corporate pension funds in the country. By virtue of their sheer size (their estimated worth at present is in the billions), they play a large part in controlling the direction of the market.

Blue chips make up what is called the Dow Jones Industrial average, which dates back to an eleven-stock average first compiled in 1884 by Charles H. Dow, editor of the *Wall Street Journal.* The Dow has since expanded to 30 stocks. The "blue chips" are the stocks of large, established companies that are recognized leaders in their respective industries. These stocks have particular appeal for the conservative investor, because the companies issuing them have demonstrated a continuing ability to make profits and pay dividends to shareholders.

More venturesome investors are often attracted to the so-called *"glamour issues."* These are the stocks of companies, usually newer or less established ones, whose prospects for future earnings are expected to be substantial. Characterized by their high Price/ Earnings (P/E) ratios — the current market share of a stock divided by the company's earnings per share over a twelve-month period — these companies sell or produce products or services for which demand is expected to increase sharply in the near future. The "glamour stock" companies tend to be trend-setters; and the investor who wants to get in on this exciting market should, by nature, be a trend watcher.

A third, and more speculative, option is investing in *"growth companies."* Often called junior companies, these are high-growth enterprises, usually involved in technologically advanced products and services, whose revenues are under $100 million. Investing in growth companies can be a risky venture, and though fortunes have been made in this sector, many a starry-eyed investor has lost out because he overpaid for expectations of high growth that never materialized. If you're going to invest in a "concept" company, it's imperative that you do your homework, which entails acquiring a working knowledge of the market for the company's product, the

127

competition, and some inside information on how the company is run and whether it has the resources and capital to cope with rapid growth. Growth stocks are not suitable for the investor who wants income, since they rarely pay a dividend.

Reading Between the Lines:
Deciphering Annual Reports and Balance Sheets

For a quick but penetrating look at a company, you can read the Standard & Poor sheets available on all major publicly traded companies. Your broker can provide them, and each is composed of a two-page condensed analysis of the company's business, its history and recent trends, and its noteworthy developments. It also offers a ten-year summary of pertinent income statement and balance sheet statistics, along with a general recommendation on whether to buy, sell or hold.

Before you plunge into stock investments, having educated yourself to some degree, you'll realize that, as in any educational process, you have to pay your tuition. Experimentation, like breakage in a school laboratory, can be costly. Unless you're unusually wary or lucky, your "tuition" will be paid in the form of occasionally losing money.

With that caution in mind, you should proceed to another area of knowledge before making any sizable forays in the investment field. How do you know which company is worthy of investment? And how do you find out the true condition of the company behind the stock that has attracted your interest?

The only way to find the answer to such a crucial question is by learning to read—or decipher—a company's annual financial report. You can get a company's annual report by writing or telephoning the corporate office directly, or your stockbroker can get it for you. Most companies are happy to send out their annual reports to potential investors. Unfortunately, to most of us, such reports are an almost trackless swamp of statistics and corporate prose.

Don't let this intimidate you. Mastering the annual report is admittedly difficult, but it's essential if you're going to become a sophisticated investor. All of the information you want and need is there; it's just that you have to do a little sorting out. Go straight for the numbers, the balance sheet, and ignore the rhetoric, which typically ranges from stilted to hip—and from murky to clear.

Most annual reports are fabulous fare, seeking to delight you with exquisite, even surrealistic, photos of products, plants and people (all of whom seem well on their way to nirvana via a parachute of purpose and productivity). More and more, in the face of competition, annual reports are becoming extravagant exercises in printing and publishing. Which isn't necessarily bad, as long as the stockholders aren't deprived of too much of their well-deserved dividends.

The balance sheet is that redoubtable section of numbers that seem somehow to end up all even, making it appear that the company itself is balanced on some sort of massive postal scale. However formidable, the balance sheet is the key to your quest, and your understanding of it will lead you out of the woods and into the light.

The main thing is not to panic and let all that fine print turn into an impenetrable blur. The thorny part of reading and evaluating a balance sheet is the specialized language of the accountants who draw it up. Once you decipher that code, you can readily grasp what it conveys of a company's status. As you can see, the balance sheet is divided into two parallel sections: on the left the assets, on the right the liabilities and stockholders' equity in the company. Under "Assets" are listed everything the company owns—plant, equipment, goods, and property—plus uncollected claims against other companies. Under "Liabilities" you see the details of the company's indebtedness, plus the total invested by its stockholders.

Here's the way the breakdown for a typical company goes. I've used our National Electrical Corporation for illustration.

NATIONAL ELECTRIC CORPORATION
Balance Sheet — June 30, 1985

	1985	1984
ASSETS		
Current Assets		
Cash	$450,000	$300,000
Marketable securities at		
cost (market value:		
1985, $890,000; 1984,		
$480,000)	850,000	460,000
Accounts receivable		
Less: allowance for		
bad debt: 1985, $100,000;		
1984, $95,000	2,000,000	1,900,000
Inventories	2,700,000	3,000,000
Total current assets	**$6,000,000**	**$5,660,000**
Fixed Assets		
Land	$450,000	$450,000
Building	3,800,000	3,600,000
Machinery	950,000	850,000
Office equipment	100,000	95,000
	$5,300,000	$4,995,000
Less: accumulated		
depreciation	1,800,000	1,500,000
Net fixed assets	**$3,500,000**	**$3,495,000**
Prepayments and deferred		
charges	100,000	90,000
Intangibles		
(goodwill, patent, trademarks) .	100,000	100,000
Total assets	**$9,700,000**	**$9,345,000**

	1985	1984
LIABILITIES		
Current liabilities		
Accounts payable	$1,000,000	$940,000
Notes payable	850,000	1,000,000
Accrued expenses payable	330,000	300,000
Federal income taxes payable	320,000	290,000
Total current liabilities	**$2,500,000**	**$2,530,000**
Long-term liabilities		
First mortgage bonds;		
5% interest, due 1995	2,700,000	2,700,000
Total liabilities	**$5,200,000**	**$5,230,000**
STOCKHOLDERS' EQUITY		
Capital stock		
Preferred stock, 5% cumulative,		
$100 par value each; autho-		
rized, issued, and oustanding		
6,000 shares	600,000	600,000
Common stock, $5 par value		
each; authorized, issued,		
and outstanding 300,000		
shares	1,500,000	1,500,000
Capital surplus	700,000	700,000
Accumulated retained earnings	1,700,000	1,315,000
Total stockholders' equity	**$4,500,000**	**$4,115,000**
Total liabilities and stockholders'		
equity	**$9,700,000**	**$9,345,000**

Assets will include cash, both in the company treasury and in its bank accounts. Marketable securities in which the company's excess or idle cash has been invested are also included—usually listed at the price paid for them, with current market value in parentheses. Under "Accounts receivable" will be found the total owed the company on products shipped to customers who are expected to pay up in 30, 60, or 90 days; against that is set a stated sum, the bad debt reserve, which is supposed to offset any accounts receivable that are defaulted. The left-hand side of the balance sheet also lists the total of the company's inventories of raw materials, goods in the process of being manufactured, and finished goods awaiting shipment.

Also itemized on the balance sheet are "fixed assets": the property occupied by the company, its plant and manufacturing equipment, office furniture and equipment, and any forms of transport owned by the company. These are valued at cost, minus the depreciation estimated to have occurred as of the date of the balance sheet. Listed as assets, too, are "prepayments." For example, the company may have paid up fire insurance for the three-year period of its premium, or paid in advance on leased or rented equipment.

Liabilities will include, first, all debts that will fall due during the coming year. Accountants will tell you that the relationship between "current assets" and "current liabilities" is a key factor in analyzing a balance sheet. Into this category fall accounts payable — the total the company owes its creditors; notes payable, the amount owed to banks and other lending sources. Another item under this heading is "accrued expenses payable," which is the money the company owes on a given day in wages paid its employees, interest on loans, attorneys' fees, insurance premiums, prensions, and the taxes due the Internal Revenue Service. Then there are long-term liabilities, all debts due after one year from the date of the balance sheet. Also on that side of the balance sheet is listed all the capital stock, preferred and common, and the paid-in capital (the total paid by shareholders over the par or legal value of each share).

Several other items on the balance sheet should command your attention.

One is "accumulated retained earnings," sometimes called "earned surplus." This amount represents earnings above the dividends the company has paid out. It's a good idea to compare this figure with those of prior years. A steady growth in retained earnings means the corporation is becoming financially stronger. Most annual reports contain a ten-year summary of the financial data, so that the most up-to-date report can give you all the information you need about prior years.

Something else to watch is the "net working capital" figure, the difference between total current assets and total current liabilities. If there is a considerable margin, this too is an indication of financial strength. According to financial analysts, *current assets should ideally be two to one over current liabilities.*

You should also check the figures showing the turnover in inventory which is defined as cost of sales divided by the latest inventory figure on the balance sheet. This ratio tells you how many times per year the company's inventory is sold. A cost of sales to inventory ratio of 2:1 is quite low, one of 10:1 quite high. This will, of course, vary greatly from industry to industry and company to company. And the sales figures for the current year should be compared with those of several previous years. Two questions to ask on this score: Have sales steadily risen? Did the company preserve a comfortable profit margin on the increased business?

The price-earnings ratio, for many investors, is of primary importance. Remember, this is calculated by dividing the market price of the stock by the earnings per share. If the stock is selling at $25 a share and earning $2 a share, the price-earnings ratio is 12½ to 1. The stock is thus said to be selling at 12½ times earnings. If the stock rose to 40, that ratio would rise to 20. A company with solid growth will probably double its earnings every five to seven years. But a decline in the price-earnings ratio is usually a cautionary signal.

You're not through yet, for the balance sheet is only one of the statements you will find in an annual report. As you have probably noticed, the balance sheet shows only the fundamental soundness of the company, but not how much money it is presently making—and without that information it's like a television set without a picture. The picture in this case is the income statement, also commonly called (for confusion's sake) a profit and loss statement, "P&L," as well as an earnings report.

By whatever name, its basic purpose is to show the operating activities of a company for an entire year so you can compare it with previous years' results. This comparison will give you some insight into whether the company is moving ahead, standing still or losing ground.

NATIONAL ELECTRIC CORPORATION
Income Statement

	1985	1984
Net sales	$11,000,000	$10,200,000
Cost of sales	8,500,000	7,959,000
Selling & general expense	1,400,000	1,325,000
Income from operations	$1,100,000	$916,000
Less: Interest expense	(135,000)	(135,000)
Other income and expenses	50,000	27,000
Income before federal income taxes	$1,015,000	$808,000
Income taxes	480,000	365,000
Net income	$535,000	$443,000

Next, we have Cost of Sales, which means all the costs incurred in the factory that go into making the product. That would be raw materials plus labor (people) and include such items as rent, electricity, supplies, maintenance and repairs.

The next item, Selling and general expense, includes two categories. Selling expense is the cost of selling the product to the customer; it includes the salaries of the people in the sales department, their travel, and associated office expense. General expense includes all the money spent for the "front office" *other* than the sales department, and that portion of the general office expense not specifically allocated to selling or the factory.

Then we get into Income from Operations, which is arrived at by the simple process of subtracting the Costs and expenses from the Net sales figure.

Any interest expense for money the company has borrowed would appear on the next line — Interest expense.

The next line shows income received by the company, aside from the sale of its product. A typical example would be dividends and interest the company earns through its investments in stocks and bonds.

The total of all the above gives us Income before taxes, and the rest of the statement is self-explanatory. The famous "bottom line" is Net income.

Analysts strongly suggest that you compare several years' results to obtain a clear picture of the company's progress or retrogression. A long backward view will show:

1. The trend of sales fluctuations.
2. The trend of earnings as compared to sales.
3. The company's reaction to general trends in the national economy.
4. The increase or decrease in return on capital.
5. Net earnings per share of common stock.
6. The company's continuing policy on dividends, whether it tends to increase such payments in ratio to increased earnings or prefers to plow the money back into the corporation as a whole.

The experts emphasize that financial statements have only half the value they should if they are "studied in a vacuum" — that is, without comparing them to those of previous years. They are your surest guide to evaluating a potential investment. Once you've mastered the art of reading and analyzing them, you'll be on your way to an aggressive investment program.

Group Investing — Is It for You?

At this point, you've mastered annual reports, perhaps attended an annual stockholders' meeting or two, and possibly done a little research into a local company. All in the interest of furthering your education. But maybe you've decided you're just not quite ready to take the leap into the stock market on your own. If so, the "togetherness" way of investing — joining an investment club — might appeal to you. The social aspect can be fun, and then there's the security afforded by numbers and group decisions.

Depending on your temperament — that is, how group-minded you are — the investment club can be a good thing. You needn't sink a lot of money into your joint ventures, and there is the fun of combined planning, the shared joy of successful investment.

I'm not a joiner myself; and I find the greatest stimulation in what I can achieve on my own. Also, I can see disadvantages in joining an investment club. There are seldom professionals directly involved, and I doubt whether the membership would be as highly venturesome as I consider myself to be.

But for many women, especially those with limited funds available for investment, the clubs constitute an excellent introduction to the financial world.

There are all sorts of groupings, some clubs having "men only" or "women only" rules, some composed of married couples, or senior citizens, or young people, or members of the same religious, social, or professional organizations. Most are affiliated with the National Association of Investment Clubs, which was founded in 1951 as a non-profit organization.

Each club, whether affiliated with the NAIC or not, decides what investments it wants to make and then calls in a broker to handle the details.

The principal idea behind the NAIC formula for group success is that all dividends and capital gains from the sale of any stock held in the club's portfolio will be reinvested rather than paid out immediately to the individual members. Members are advised to invest a certain sum each month and withdraw any accumulated holdings only in an emergency. A member can invest a $10 unit per month—the usual minimum—or several units of $10 each, but generally a maximum is set to prevent wealthier members from dominating a group.

Some clubs operate through an investment committee with a chairman and several members, the make-up of which is rotated every three or four months. This committee evaluates several growth stocks each month. The committee reports on its evaluations at the monthly meetings, and the membership votes on whether to follow the committee's recommendations. Many clubs also have a portfolio management committee, which reports monthly on the current value of each stock held by the club.

Since most people join investment clubs that are affiliated with the NAIC, it might be helpful to you in deciding whether to join such a group to know what the association recommends for its affiliates. The NAIC suggests that investments be made on a regular basis, regardless of the fluctuations of the market; if it's down, and the club's portfolio has accordingly depreciated, you will keep investing $10, $20, or whatever each month. All earnings should be reinvested to compound the portfolio's value. Investments should be diversified among various companies and industries. The main emphasis is on buying growth stocks (ones that increase in value faster than the economy as a whole).

Naturally the success of the clubs varies, depending on the combined acumen of their memberships. They can provide the social excitement of the shared risk. Put more bluntly, you don't feel quite so bad about losing money if a number of other people have suffered equally. The other side of the coin is that you can all rejoice together when things are going well. The socializing, I suspect, is half the fun of the investment clubs. Certainly they provide an opportunity for women without a lot to venture, or who are cautious and conservative by nature.

Mutual Funds: The Multi-Purpose Investment

Another way of togetherness investing, which combines some of the benefits of the investment club (minimal initial investment and lower risk) with the elements of greater scope and possibility *and* professional management, is the mutual fund. Because it is difficult to predict the behavior of any particular stock, or even to forecast trends in the stock market, mutual funds were first established to take some of the risk out of stock ownership. Essentially a professionally managed portfolio of many different stocks and/or bonds, the theory behind the mutual fund is that if the risk is spread over a wide range of companies and industries, one company's disaster or an industry downturn won't have a significant effect on the worth of a fund owner's shares.

Mutual funds have been touted as *"the* investment of the '80s."* The main advantage of mutual funds over other "liquid" investments is that they provide an opportunity for many people to do collectively what they could not possibly do on their own. The *raison d'etre* for mutual funds is primarily economical: hiring a competent investment manager to manage a fund for thousands of investors who have essentially the same goal (growth, income, build-up of retirement assets, etc.) is less expensive than having each of those investors hire a broker who will, hopefully, place their investable cash in a variety of stocks and monitor them on a regular basis.

The primary advantage of mutual funds is, of course, diversification. Most investors who want to get into the stock market simply do not have the sum required (most experts peg it at around $200,000) to diversify enough to keep risk at a safe, even manageable, level. That's the most important task of the professional fund manager. He or she is required by law to exercise "due diligence" and work for the best interests of the investors: and that due diligence entails doing more in-depth research and constant monitoring than the individual investor is likely to have the time and expertise to conduct.

A special attraction of mutual funds for the first-time investor is that you can actually start an investment portfolio with as little as *$100*: It's not much, but if it gets you on the road to increasing your net worth, that investment—added to monthly—should give you a good feeling. Another benefit is that it costs little, and sometimes nothing if you choose a "no-load" (no commission) fund, to buy or sell your shares.

Aside from professional management, liquidity, low fees and diversification, there's another advantage to mutual funds: The relative safety of the assets. By law, the fund's assets must be held by a third party, usually a bank or trust company, who provide whatever control is necessary in the transfer and distribution of the funds.

Types of Mutual Funds
Shopping for mutual funds is like being in the women's wear department of Bloomingdale's. There's one to suit an investor of virtually any style or temperament, and they come in all shapes and sizes. Essentially, however, there are about a half-dozen types of mutual funds—each designed to suit a different goal.

The Growth Funds
Sometimes called capital gains, performance or capital appreciation funds, the goal of growth funds is to produce capital gains rather than current income.

The *performance* funds are the "movers and shakers" of the growth mutual fund group. They are aggressively managed, sometimes speculative, and as such involve more risk than other types of funds. The portfolio of these funds often comprises small or new companies, high-tech or "breakthrough product" companies, and companies with low P/E (price to earnings) ratios.

Clearly for the sophisticated investor, performance funds

offer the opportunity to get in on high-potential investments and yet spread the risk through diversification. A novice investor might consider switching shares into these funds on an occasional basis — just to get a feel for higher-risk investing. Some of these funds will soar and some will sink, but overall, you can probably expect that when the market starts a downward slide, chances are the performance funds won't be far behind.

Straight-growth funds soft-shelled, slow-and-steady versions of the growth fund. The emphasis here is on moderate, long-term growth, and the holdings are usually invested in the large well-known corporations with reputations for good, steady growth. The prospectus of a growth fund might define the fund's objective as "to seek capital growth consistent with . . . prudent risk" which, roughly translated, means that the fund will invest in "safe" stocks expected to increase in value over time. The growth fund stocks often pay a dividend, though it will probably be slightly less than the going market rate because growing companies tend to allot a large portion of their cash flow for future development.

Because of their more conservative management, straight-growth funds aren't as volatile as the performance funds. These funds will follow the market trends, too, but some of the good ones outperform the market as a whole when times are good and tend to suffer only moderate losses on the down side. If you're willing as an investor to assume some risk in hopes of greater gain — and you earmark these funds for long-term goals — straight-growth funds are a good choice.

Income funds, as the name implies, aim to give investors the highest current yield the stock market has to offer. If you invest in these funds, you may have to pay capital gains occasionally, but the emphasis is on giving you spendable cash on a regular basis and keeping your capital investment intact. The yield on these funds needs to be carefully watched, as keeping capital intact and receiving a small income from your investment is often not enough to keep up with inflation and cost of living increases. As these funds are ultraconservative and their yields are often less than money funds, they shouldn't play a significant part in your overall investment strategy.

Bond funds are designed to provide long-term high yields. They are pegged to interest rates and therefore often deliver short-term capital losses in periods of escalating interest rates. Funds whose holdings are invested in municipal bonds publicize their federal tax-free status as a selling point and while tax savings are a factor in any investment, your primary concern should always be the yield.

Despite the fact that these funds, like the income funds, are considered ultraconservative investments, they can play an essential part in your overall money management plan. That's because, in the long run even with a relatively stable economy, interest rates are bound to fluctuate. If, as predicted, we continue to see a slow but steady decline in interest rates, bond funds will eventually pay off. William Donahue, in his excellent book, *No-load Mutual Fund Guide*, advises placing at least five percent of your capital in these funds as "catastrophe insurance," in the event of a depression.

Money funds emphasize liquidity and, like their counterpart, money market accounts, can be used as a place to park cash while evaluating other investments. The two types of money funds include the government securities funds, in which holdings are invested strictly in U.S. Government-backed Treasury bills and/or other federal agency obligations, and the tax-free money funds. These are essentially a combination of money market investments and short-term municipal bonds and notes; their tax-free status gives them special appeal for investors in very high tax brackets. If safety is a prime consideration, the government-only funds provide a sort of trade-off: The few percentage points you may lose in yield may be offset by the emotional security gained.

Some money funds require a minimum investment of as little as $250, though the range is usually between $250 and $1000.

Because of their diversifications, money funds provide slightly higher yields and more safety than an individual investment in the money market. A prime advantage of these funds is their instant liquidity; if you want to withdraw your money, you can simply write yourself a check or telephone the fund (most have toll-free numbers) and ask them to wire your money to you.

Mutual funds have changed a great deal since I wrote the first version of this book. I now believe that they have a place in every investor's portfolio, as time has shown that they have performed well over the distance. Chances are you won't make a killing in mutuals, but you probably won't be wiped out, either. And because of the range of possibilities in mutual funds, they could feasibly satisfy some of your short- and long-term goals and give you a stepping stone to some more aggressive investing.

11
Aggressive Money and Other Investment Ventures

Let's say you've filled in most of the lower blocks in your Financial Planning Pyramid by now. You've stashed four to six months' income in a savings account. You have adequate personal insurance and own your own house; you've picked up a few Treasury bills or certificates of deposit. If being part of an investment club or a mutual fund nest egg holds no charms for you and you're determined to win your economic independence through your own efforts, you'll already have given serious thought to entering the field of aggressive money. That's where the creative action is. You should remember, however, that stocks and the stock market are in fact aggressive investments and should not be entered until all the bottom blocks of your pyramid are filled in. All too often people want to start in by taking a flier in the market — and very rarely do they make it.

Don't neglect your reading: the *Wall Street Journal, Barron's, Forbes,* for *Business Week,* the financial pages of the *New York Times* and other leading papers. Most financial publications write about exciting things that aggressive business people have *made* happen. By this time, too, you'll have mastered the supposedly esoteric terminology of the market and the various strategies for increasing your net worth through risk investment rather than saving. You'll also have picked up some of the intense competitive joy of winning your place in the market, of managing your own money and therefore your future independence.

All the jargon will now be as familiar to you as the names of the standard brands in the supermarket. You'll know that when people refer to the day's DJIA or "Dow," it's the Dow Jones Industrial Average—a function of the prices of a certain 30 companies' stocks that day—which is the oldest indicator of how the market is moving as a whole, the key figure mentioned in newspaper headlines and nightly television news programs. This is a hotly contested subject. Is the performance of 30 stocks out of thousands a true indicator? Well, it *is* an indicator, and one to be watched just because it's there. You should recognize that the Dow Jones Industrial Average is not the most representative average of the market as a whole. Newer and more all-inclusive averages have been developed more recently, such as the New York Stock Exchange Composite Index and the *Standard and Poor's 500*, both much broader than the 30 industrials included in the DJIA. However, long history and popularity still make the DJIA the most widely quoted and used index among members of the investing public.

You'll know the difference between "bid" and "asked," bid being the highest price anyone is offering for a certain stock, asked being the lowest price at which anyone is willing to sell it at a given time. That "averaging up" means buying more of a certain issue as its price goes up, and "averaging down" means buying more of that issue as its price falls. That "book value" signifies the net worth that backs up a company's common stock (stockholders' equity divided by number of common shares outstanding). That "dollar stocks" are low-price, highly speculative issues. That "buying on margin" means buying listed stocks by making a down payment — the amount regulated by the Federal Reserve Bank — on the full price of a stock, the balance being borrowed from your brokerage at a certain interest rate. That "preferred stock" is one on which a company must pay dividends before doing so on common stock. That "daily quotations," as published in your newspaper's financial section, refers to the previous day's highest, lowest, and closing prices paid for stocks on the various exchanges.

By then, too, you'll understand just how the trading process works, from the moment you phone your broker with a decision to buy a certain stock to the moment the transaction is completed. The stock exchange works the same way as an auction market.

Let's say that you've decided, after consultation with your broker, to buy 100 shares of National Electric (a fictitious corporation). He'll probably push a button on the console on his desk to receive a reading on a screen showing that the last sale of National Electric was at 44½, meaning $44.50 a share. You agree to buy it at that price, or he may suggest that you place an order for the stock at a slightly lower quotation, 44-3/8, to "see if we get any bids," this being a "good till cancelled order." Or he may place a "day order," which means the price you bid is good for that day only, and if that price isn't reached in the day's trading it would have to be renewed the following day.

Your order for 100 shares of National Electric then goes to the brokerage's order room, from which it is telegraphed to the firm's head office in New York, if it has one, or to the broker's representative on the floor of the New York Stock Exchange.

A clerk receives the order and turns it over to the floor broker, who heads immediately for the appropriate trading post. The nearly 2,000 stocks listed on the new York Stock Exchange are divided up among its 22 trading posts. Let's say National Electric is traded at Post 7. At this station the floor broker with your order joins a group of men — often shouting or gesturing violently —

gathered around a "specialist," a broker wearing a special jacket who specializes in trading National Electric and a small number of other stocks. It is the specialist's function to make an "orderly market" in the stocks for which he has responsibility. That means that he keeps an order book in which he enters both the bids to buy the stock and any offers to sell the stock, and matches buyers with sellers at prices on which they can both agree.

In those cases where the bid and the ask prices are so far apart that a potential buyer and seller cannot get together and agree on a price, it is the specialist's function to purchase or sell the stock for his own personal account at a price somewhere between the most recent bid and ask prices, and thus personally to create what is referred to as an "orderly market." The function of the specialist is presently a very controversial subject, and the next several years may bring fundamental changes in this area.

The specialist quotes to your broker's representative the going price for the stock. If you've instructed your broker to place a market order — that is, at the current quotation — his representative will tell the specialist he wants 100 shares at that price. If, on the other hand, you and your broker have decided to place a "good till canceled order" or a "day order," the specialist will note the price you're willing to pay in his notebook and fill the order if and when the price reaches the level you've designated.

Word that your order has been filled is telegraphed to your broker. Often within an hour you will be informed that you are the owner of 100 shares of National Electric. You then have five working days in which to give your broker a check to complete the transaction.

These, in brief, are the mechanics of buying a stock listed on one of the major exchanges. It's a little different in dealing with over-the-counter (OTC) stocks, which represent companies generally not yet mature or successful enough to be traded on one of the major exchanges. Major exceptions include American Express and many large banks, which are traded OTC (over the counter).

Say you're interested in an OTC stock selling for around $12 a share. You call your broker and ask for the current quotations. It's a good thing to remember that the spread between "bid" and "ask" price in the OTC market is generally a lot wider than on the American or New York Stock Exchange issues. Your broker may tell you the bid is 11-7/8 for the stock you're interested in, and the asking price is 12¼. That's a big spread. That means the people owning the stock are willing to sell it for $12.25 while people buying the stock are willing to pay $11.87 a share. If your broker places an order with a ceiling of 12-1/8 or $12.13, the chances are excellent that you will be able to buy it at the compromise price. The less frequently traded an OTC stock is, the wider the spread between the bid and ask prices.

One drawback to dealing over the counter is the larger spread. It is also customary for some over-the-counter dealers to buy and sell certain stocks for their own account. Often the profit or spread they make on such transactions, or the commission they charge on OTC transactions, is greater than a commission in a New York Stock Exchange transaction would be.

There are so many struggling for their share of the available capital to expand and eventually to reach Big Board status that the OTC market, in aggregate, is many times larger than that of the major exchanges. Many of the fastest growth businesses have their stocks sold over the counter. Often, too, the OTC stocks represent long-entrenched and conservatively managed companies operating only in a certain locality or region. Such localized concerns might include banks, water and power companies, machine shops, bus lines, and a whole range of commerce and industry that is too remote or obscure to attract the attention of Wall Street. You might say they comprise the minor leagues of finance, but many dramatic successes have emerged from their ranks.

Many women inexperienced in the ways of the financial world have asked me, "But isn't buying stocks just like playing the crap tables at Las Vegas?" They've heard of the speculative side of stock investment, of paper fortunes made and lost, of people "ruined" in the 1929 crash because they'd bought stocks on margin and had to sell everything they owned to pay what they owed a broker for buying stocks with a ten percent down payment and the balance borrowed from the broker.

The days of reckless speculation in margin accounts are over; at this writing the Securities and Exchange Commission has set the margin level at 50 percent to discourage such headlong dicing. (Even so, margin purchases still remain a problem; when margin calls went out during a recent market break, a lot of people got hurt. Be wary of the broker who urges a lot of people got hurt. Be wary of the broker who urges a lot of margin action.) But you could hardly call buying quality stocks or collecting dividends "gambling." Whatever the rise or fall of a stock's market price, you still own those shares and receive the dividends on them. Naturally, you can lose money if you sell the stock at a lower price than you paid for it. If you hang on to it until its value has recovered (if it does), you've suffered only a paper loss during the period the stock is in decline.

As G.M. Loeb has written in perhaps the best book dealing with the stock market, *The Battle for Investment Survival* (first published in 1935 but reprinted many times since and still fresh and valid):

> Accepting losses is the most important single investment device to insure safety of capital. It is also the action that most people know the least about and that they are least liable to execute. . . .
> The most important single thing I have learned is that accepting losses promptly is the first key to success.

In other words, when the stock drops below your buy price, don't let it ride in hopes of its going back up. Cut your losses fast — sell!

Mr. Loeb, whose immense authority was derived from half a

century in the money game and a senior partnership in E.F. Hutton and Company, exemplifies what I mean about "aggressive money," the determination to make money work for you and provide a secure, comfortable future. To be aggressive in the money sense, you have to be resilient enough to accept losses and failures, certain in the knowledge that this is the only way you're going to liberate yourself financially.

And he sums up exactly what I define as the method of running aggressive money:

Aim at a real profit. Reject everything that does not promise to advance generously in price. *Keep cash* if enough issues cannot be found or if the investment per issue becomes unwieldly. Shares purchased for a big profit may be sold long before the original goal is achieved. . . . *Keep uninvested* unless and until a particularly opportune time presents itself. . . . Nevertheless, mistakes will be made. And when they are, there is no cheaper insurance than accepting a loss quickly. . . .

The only way to succeed in venturesome management of your money is by creatively using the generating power of that money and constantly analyzing the results. You can't think of your capital as an egg waiting to be hatched by others. Money is now your avocation, if not your vocation; as such, it has to be given the same kind of personal attention a mother devotes to her children. The more mental energy you put into your money management — the more analyzing and studying and investigating you do, the more time you spend reading the *Wall Street Journal* and financial pages, observing the fluctuations of the market in the flyspeck print of the day's Wall Street quotations — the quicker you will free yourself from the gritty concerns of paying bills, sweating over budgets and worrying about inflation. You can avoid such daily afflictions and make your life a lot more fun, by creatively using the generating power of money intelligently invested.

Which brings me to the sad story of a friend of mine. Several years ago she sold a house and realized a tidy profit on the transaction. She decided to invest the money in stock, felt attracted to Technicolor, Inc., and learned that it was selling for only $7 a share.

Right after she bought 3,000 shares at 7 there was a boom in Technicolor film production, and the stock began to soar. When it reached 26, she decided to bail out, her holdings having almost quadrupled in value. (Actually she'd have made a bigger killing if she'd held on to the stock a bit longer; it went up into the 40s. But it's always better to sell too soon than too late.)

What happened was that Maggie suffered from an attack of overoptimism. It was the mid-sixties, the economy was surging forward and the economists were all talking confidently about how they'd arranged permanent prosperity for the country. Instead of working at building up her investment portfolio, Maggie carelessly distributed her capital in a number of undistinguished stocks and took off for Europe. With everything booming, one stock seemed as good as another; it was out-of-sight, out-of-mind time. She enjoyed herself so much in Europe that after she'd returned home she decided to travel in the other direction and make it around the world.

Maggie was in the Punjab when she got the bad news from Wall Street. The bottom had dropped out of her stocks, along with a lot of others. It was back to reality for Maggie—and back to work, too. You take a cavalier attitude toward money at your peril.

Eternal vigilance isn't only the price of liberty; it's the gate toll to solvency and self-realization. You *must* keep studying, analyzing, changing your position if necessary; never, never take the market for granted.

Actually there's a sequel to Maggie's tragic tale, and it's every bit as instructive. Because she had risen to fortune on Technicolor, Inc., she developed an emotional attachment to that stock—not as odd a phenomenon as you might think. For no good reason she bought back into it after she'd raised some capital again — and let herself be hoodwinked into reinvesting every time she would sell something. You must learn to say no: If you've decided to sell out, *do it* and pick up the money. Don't be conned into reinvesting in another stock — by yourself, or by your broker.

The generative power of money is something that women in the past have sometimes found difficult to grasp. All too often money means a thin sheaf of currency in the purse, or figures noted in a bank's checkbook. Something inert, lifeless, static. Something, in effect, to be ignored until you need it to pay for the groceries or for a fling in Barbados (or, worse yet, something that isn't there when you need it).

To illustrate this "generative power" I'm talking about, a celebrated New York banker years ago made an interesting projection, based on the fact that capital compounded at five percent doubles itself in a little more than fourteen years. If the wealthy Medici family in Italy six centuries ago had set aside, at five percent compound interest, an investment fund equal to $100,000, by 1933 that fund would have increased in value to $517,000,000,000,000, 000 ($517 quadrillion), or 46 million times the existing monetary gold supply in the whole world.

I'm not suggesting that you set your mind on founding a Medici-type dynasty, but you should be aware of the fact that only through investment can you protect yourself against the greater threat to preserving your capital — the constant variation in the purchasing power of money caused by such factors as inflation, taxation, government regulation, war, changes in the political and economic climate, and social unrest.

Creative investment is your way, in essence, of protecting what you've worked for, saved, worried over. And you are protecting your family as well. It isn't an expression of greed, or wanting to snatch what others have, or merely "money-grubbing," as the lazy and envious like to call it.

You have to observe a stock's behavior much as you watch over and correct a child's conduct to make sure he/she doesn't slip into delinquency.

Once you've bought stock in a company, you should keep careful tabs on its dividends policy. Dividends are not always consistent, and dividend policy varies, of course, from company to company. When you bought the stock, you were probably told it had paid, say $10 a year for the past years. But you can't count on getting $10 annually for every share you own. Some companies stick like bonding glue to their proclaimed dividend rate and regard it as something sacrosanct, not to be affected by a slump in business or other disasters. Others will decide, in board meetings in which you have not part, that the dividend must be lowered for a certain year, or skipped altogether if the company's financial situation is suffering.

You'll have to keep an eye on your investment to determine just how faithful the company is about paying out dividends.

And if dividend payments become erratic over the course of a few years, you should take a hard look at whether or not to keep your money tied up in that company's future.

Many companies, as you may find out too late if you're counting on strictly cash dividends, pay off in shares of stock, or a mixture of cash and stock. This is often true of growing companies that want to hold on to their cash reserves and use them for expansion or increased operating expenses.

Though people often feel they are getting a break through stock dividends, they really may not be. Suppose you hold 100 shares in our mythical National Electric for which you paid $45 a share, or a total of $4,500. If National Electric declares a five percent stock dividend, and you thus receive five more shares of the company, that doesn't mean you've received the equivalent of $225. You now have 105 shares instead of 100, but your total investment is still $4500 and your holdings still represent the same percentage of ownership in the company as your 100 shares did.

You'll stand to gain, of course, if the price of the company's stock does not drop because of the stock dividend.

A stock split is different from a stock dividend, though the two are closely related. Again the benefit is more psychological than mathematical; but the shareholders in a growth company like the splits because they are usually performed by companies whose earning are on the rise, and they are taken as a sign that the company is really growing.

Suppose National Electric announces a two-for-one stock split. Your 100 shares are increased to 200. But they still represent the same percentage of ownership in the company. The market value per share of your stock usually is halved when a stock split is announced. Sometimes it is a little more than half, and you have a margin of profit, on paper, further increased if investors push up the price.

The close relationship between stock dividends and stock splits is indicated by the fact that the New York Stock Exchange considers anything less than a 20 percent stock distribution a dividend; anything over that figure a stock split. Many brokers and analysts contend that there is a built-in psychological factor here—that stock-splitting draws in a lot of investors who feel they're picking up a bargain, "getting one the ground floor."

What should be included in your portfolio? That can be answered only in generalizations, since all of us differ in age, education, career possibilities, and earned or inherited income; no woman's situation is exactly like another's.

If your circumstances dictate a conservative approach, you'll naturally want a mixture of stocks and bonds that guarantee a steady income. Most career women, fairly young and with good prospects, will or should want to be more adventurous. Even those with family responsibilities, many experts now believe, should take a more aggressive attitude toward managing their capital.

You should manage your own portfolio, of course, unless your holdings are so large that they require a professional, in which case you probably wouldn't be reading this book. Use your own judgment, based on study and research. Don't invest all your money in a few stocks, but aim for a mix. Keep careful records of how each stock performs so that you'll be up to the minute on their prospects in the market.

Experts generally agree that there are several guidelines to be followed by practically all investors with fair-sized portfolios. (This would not apply if you're just venturing into the money world and have only a few thousand dollars to invest.)

1. You should have about 20 to 25 percent of your portfolio invested in "good" stocks with steady track records.

2. A cash reserve is advisable for purchase of bargains in the market that might crop up suddenly.

3. You *don't* always have to be in the game. If making money in a particular market is unlikely, you should just get out and lie low until another opportunity arises. (You always need to be evaluating your investments in terms of the risk-reward ratio. For instance, when interest rates are high, people tend to stay out of the market. The reason for this is that you can get safer—and perhaps equivalent—returns from Treasury bills, Certificates of Deposit, and so on.)

4. Make sure your holdings are growing in value. You should expect a percent increase in general value (appreciation plus dividends) on the sounder stocks annually, a percent rate on the more speculative ones — at least when the market is trending upward.

That way your little golf go-cart will keep up with or gain on that 11 m.p.h. conveyor belt. And that is the object of the game. A woman may learn that nothing is much more stimulating—to her mind, her career, or her future—than aggressive money handling. If she's skillful, she can make it all the way.

Investment Adventures

For only the most sophisticated and daring among investors there is a method of speculation called *options*. It consists of three different concepts, mysteriously called *calls, puts,* and *straddles*. These are all various types of options that have totally different functions. The options market has been around for over a century, but has recently taken on new popularity and interest. However, no beginner should venture into this area, nor should anyone with a limited amount of capital who can't afford to take high risks. We're on the summit of that financial planning pyramid now, where the winds are violent and the footing precarious. Options are not for the conservative or faint of heart.

Generally these offshoots of the stock market deal with options to buy or sell common stocks at predetermined prices. You're betting, in effect, on the future rise or fall of the price of the underlying stock.

A *call* is an option to buy 100 shares of a stock, usually listed on the New York Stock Exchange, at a prearranged price within a certain period (usually several months). The buyer of a call is therefore betting the stock will rise. A *put* is just the opposite: an option to sell that stock at a certain price. The buyer expects the stock to drop so he can buy it in the open market at a price less than his put price. The third option is termed a *straddle*, which is a simultaneous put and call. Therefore, the straddle buyer is betting that the stock will go either up or down *sharply*; in either case he makes money.

This is the way it works: You pay a small amount of money called a *premium* for a much larger amount of stock than is represented by the premium. You don't actually own the stock, merely an option on buying or selling it. You choose whether and when to exercise the option. If the stock doesn't move in the direction you thought it would, you simply drop the option and lose the premium, a matter perhaps of a few hundred dollars. One advantage of puts and calls is that you know exactly how much you stand to lose—the premium only; another is that they can be used to hedge your stock holdings in a falling market.

For sophisticated investors, such option trading is becoming undeniably more attractive, so attractive that there is now the Chicago Board Options Exchange (CBOE), a market that deals only in options to buy or sell stock. A similar service has also been provided by the American Stock Exchange.

Since I haven't dealt in stock options myself, I can only quote the CBOE's claim that it "streamlines the processing of options trades" and accomplishes a "breakthrough" by creating "a secondary market in which holders and writers of CBOE options should be able to transfer their interest in an option contract at a price that reflects the amount of time it still has to run." Until recently, the Chicago exchange explains, "options have been dealt in without the availability of such a secondary market," but now a "call option takes on the attributes of a full-fledged security whose market characteristics should resemble those of a short-term warrant."

A warrant, considered the most conservative type of option, can be described as a long-term "call." It is an option to buy a stock at a specific price over a long period of time (vs. a call which is short term), in some cases an indefinite period of time. Warrants often grow out of initial stock or bond offerings.

The CBOE is candid in stating that its offerings aren't for everyone:

> If your approach to stock investing is to hold stocks for extended periods either for their dividend yield or anticipated long-term growth, then the purchase of options probably doesn't mesh with your objectives (except for sophisticated hedging uses). The "writing" of options (the opposite of buying an option) can be employed in a conservative, yield-oriented course of investment, but option writing typically involves considerable

stock turnover for which some investors may not
be attuned.

In other words, look out for trap doors, deadfalls, spring guns and
elephant pits.

The CBOE also cautions that "an option is a 'wasting asset'
and that, secondary market or not, a call option's value will
decline to zero at its expiration unless the price of the underlying
stock is in excess of the option's exercise price." Yes, that's zero.
On the other hand, the secondary market, which is the CBOE's
innovation, "makes possible at least the partial recovery of the
premium paid for an option in instances where it appears, in
advance of the otpion's expiration date, that the price of the stock
is not headed for the anticipated rise."

One possible investing maneuver is to make a "short sale" of a
stock while holding a call option on the stock. (A short sale is
selling, by borrowing, a stock you don't own in hopes that its price
will drop, at which point you can buy at the lower price, making a
profit on the difference. It is, in effect, the other side of a normal
"long" stock transaction.)

You've got the idea. If speculation is your thing, the options
market will give you plenty of action. But you are buying only
options – not the stock itself, which is a solid asset.

Another highly speculative operation is buying contracts for
commodity futures. That is, you gamble on the future price of
such commodities as wheat, corn, sugar, copper, soybeans, cocoa,
even pork bellies. These, of course, are subject to such uncontroll-
able factors as the wind and weather, insect plagues, droughts,
fertilizer and oil shortages, revolutions and nationalizations of
foreign companies in unstable countries. You buy a "futures"
contract for delivery of a certain commodity; the contract can be
sold before the delivery date. To buy the contract you make a
down payment of ten to twenty percent of the purchase price, plus
broker's commissions and clearinghouse fees.

As in the stock options market, one attraction of buying

commodity futures is that the down payment is small, and you can either sell your holdings before the delivery date or take delivery, which means you'll have to pay storage costs on the commodity you've bought. Naturally most people sell before delivery and control the commodity only on paper in hopes of making a profit on its resale if the price of the commodity rises.

Obviously you should know a lot about the commodity you choose to speculate on: how it's produced, the climatic factors, the politics of the country it comes from, the market shifts that might produce a shortage in, say, wheat which would result in an upward trend of prices. For example: Cocoa was in short supply between 1966 and 1969, and the price rose dramatically; in 1973 the Russian wheat purchase shot up the price on those commodity futures. Fine. But predicting such events takes a lot more than a crystal ball or a reliance on hunches. And even then it is, as the securities experts say, "shooting the rapids."

If the commodities market seems alluring to you, it's a good idea to practice first on paper, like making mental bets on horse races. Pick out a commodity, pretend to buy futures in it, and see how well you've done. (That way, you'll at least remain decently clothed and fed.) It is enormously challenging to the experienced speculator. Your daily newspaper may, and the *Wall Street Journal* does, carry a complete record of commodity contract prices every day. By studying these tables you can, from day to day, find out how well you would have done had you actually bought or sold a particular commodity contract.

12

The Gilt-edged World

The term "gilt-edged" is often applied to debentures and bonds, not only because of the elaborate imitation gold-leaf scrollwork that adorned them in former days, but because this type of security is considered very safe. Bonds may be boring compared to stocks, but many investors would rather be safe than sorry. They are government or corporate IOUs, a promise on the part of the issuer to repay the amount invested by a certain date, in return for which you receive regular interest payments. Bonds are not 100 percent safe, however, since the company, municipality, or utility can, in fact, go bankrupt.

During the high inflation period of the late '70s and early '80s bonds were out of favor because their relatively low returns simply couldn't keep pace with escalating inflation rates. Gold and real estate were the darlings of that era, but as inflation began to correct itself bonds not only came back into favor but have proven to be real winners in the past few years.

Many experts maintain that there is a place for bonds in everyone's portfolio, regardless of the condition of the economy. Obviously, you'll do better wish your bond investments when inflation is low. I feel, though, that bonds can play an important part in your planning and investments at any time—especially with the advent of the new forms of bonds, many of which offer tax advantages in addition to solid returns. (See Chapter 10 for a description of the "new" bonds.)

What's the difference between a stock and a bond? A stockholder is in effect a part owner of a company in which he has invested. A bondholder is a creditor of the company whose investment is usually secured by a specific asset pledged for this purpose, such as real estate, rolling stock, and so on. This secures the creditor in case the company has difficulty in paying off the bond when it matures. If a company goes broke, the bondholders are paid off before the stockholders. Since the latter take the larger risk, they may expect a larger return on their investment.

A *debenture* is an unsecured bond, a corporation's long-term promissory note. It is not secured by a specific asset but is an unsecured general obligation of the company. Like a bondholder, the owner of a debenture is the creditor of the issuing company and cannot vote on company business, as a stockholder does. A *convertible debenture* is somewhat different—I'll discuss it later on in this chapter.

Bonds and debentures are not particularly attractive to me, as compared with stocks, because they are not an aggressive form of investment. I tend to agree with G.M. Loeb that

> ... bonds of any grade are only occasionally useful in the informed investor's portfolio. . . . It is difficult to get advice on them. Bond houses usually concentrate in the issues on their shelves. Brokers find the commission too low and are too busy to give them careful study for the negligible remuneration.

Yet bonds are powerfully attractive to some investors, and there are several hundred specialists in bond sales throughout the country who find buyers for billions of dollars' worth of such securities every year.

The prices of issued and outstanding bonds fluctuate for various reasons, but the overall trend of the bond market is primarily determined by long-term interest rate levels. If the interest rates offered by new bond issues are rising, prices of older bond issues drop to equalize the return offered. If long-term interest rates are heading down, however, outstanding bonds become much more attractive to the investor since their prices are rising.

The problem with bonds (as with many other investments) is that their after-tax yield may not keep pace with inflation. For example: Let's say an eight percent bond is selling at face value. The taxpayer is in the 30 percent bracket. Her after-tax net yield is 5.6 percent (70 percent of eight percent). If inflation is running at, say, nine percent per year, she is losing purchasing power at the rate of 3.4 percent per year. Bad news, over the long run.

Nevertheless, bonds are one of the most popular instruments of debt financing for cities, utilities, and major companies. And bonds do differ widely—which is why they are rated by a coding system in *Moody's* and *Standard and Poor*. The rating system runs from AAA (best) down to A; then BBB ranging down to B. Mr. Loeb's advice is to buy only AAA bonds; otherwise (and I agree) you are running a risk equivalent to investing in a stock without any upside potential because bonds are set at a fixed return, and stocks are of course open-ended.

This is roughly how the bond market works:

Our favorite example, National Electric Corporation, is selling bonds at $1,000 each, with a fixed interest rate of eight percent, or $80 per year. If interest rates rise and National Electric's rivals in the bond market begin offering new bonds at ten percent interest or $100 a year, those older National Electric bonds could drop in market value to about $800. At that lower price National Electric's fixed interest payment, still $80 per year, would amount to a current yield of ten percent for every person who bought a bond at $800.

If a bondholder keeps the bond until it matures — that is, until the date it must be paid off — he will get $1,000 back from the issuer in addition to the interest he receives every year until it matures. Thus the "yield to maturity" — taking into account the final repayment of the bond itself — will be different from the "current yield," represented by the interest alone. A woman who bought a National Electric $1,000 bond for $800 on a temporarily declining market, therefore, would have a $200 capital gain *plus* the annual interest at maturity.

There are three general types of bonds on the market:

1. *Corporate* bonds, issued by business firms.
2. *Municipal* bonds, issued by local and state governments to finance various projects.
3. *U.S. government* bonds, which are direct obligations of the Treasury, and other federal issues offered separately by government agencies.

All types of bonds, in fact, are issued to raise money for certain purposes. The American Telephone and Telegraph Company will float a bond issue to expand the telephone system. Your own city government will issue bonds to build, say, a new sewage disposal plant. Both private companies and government agencies usually would have been able to borrow money from the banks, but for various reasons they often find it less costly to enter the bond market for the capital they require.

The bond market may seem to be one of the more staid sectors of the money world, but it does a brisk business. Every day, up to a dozen new corporate and municipal bond issues are offered the investing public. And that's in addition to a constant turnover in older issues.

A good proportion of the issues are bought by various institutions, but there's plenty of action left for the private investor. Bond-buying is heavily favored by insurance companies, banks, credit unions, mutual funds, pension funds and labor unions, which tend to invest large amounts of money in the more conservative securities.

It's the safety factor that attracts all that money which has to be diverted, often by law, to the sure-thing kind of investment. That sure-thing factor, too, would influence you if, say, your husband is incapacitated or there is serious illness in your family, or you're a widowed or divorced mother with children. If not, you'll be looking for a higher rate of return on your money.

The institutional investors, burdened with responsibilities as they are, operate cautiously even in the safety zone represented by the bond market. Some institutions are required by law to invest only in government or muncipal bonds, while insurance companies generally favor corporate bonds because they offer a higher return. Since securities issued by the U.S. government are regarded as the safest of all bonds, they offer a lower interest rate. On bonds issued by state or local governments, the interest is usually lower than that on federal government or corporate bonds, but they have an important fringe benefit: there is no federal tax payable on the interest from municipal bonds, and usually there is no state income tax payable on bonds issued in the state of the bondholder's residence. If a taxpayer is in the 50 percent bracket and purchases a municipal bond with a five percent interest coupon, this is equivalent to interest on a regular bond paying ten percent, since half of that interest would be payable in federal income taxes. The actual return (after taxes) is therefore higher than it is for federal issues. This may change when the next tax bill comes into effect, so be sure to check with your advisor before buying bonds.

What are the comparative rates of interest offered by various types of bonds? They fluctuate to some degree, depending on the state of the bond market. The readings for a recent day will give you some idea of their returns. High-quality corporate bonds were offering 8.4 percent annual interest—less than the rate of inflation—while federal government issues were paying 6.25 percent and state or municipal bonds 6.01 percent.

There is a considerable spread in the interest rates offered by corporate bond issues and, of equal importance to the prospective investor, is the financial soundness of the companies issuing them.

A good rule of thumb: The larger and stronger company is a safer investment than a struggling concern — but it will also yield a lower return in interest.

You can find out just how safe a corporate bond is by consulting one of several independent credit rating services that assess new bond issues with the same cold practiced eye as a loan officer surveying an applicant for a personal loan. A triple-A rating is given those companies with the soundest financial structure. The least favorable assessment is a C rating. In between are a half-dozen other classifications. Your broker can give you complete information on the bond rating by *Standard and Poor* or *Moody's*.

There are several interesting ventures in the federal sector of the bond market; you may have heard about them if you travel with people who favor that kind of investment. One is called "Fannie Maes," and even their Wall Street nickname makes them attractive to fairly conservative investors.

Fannie Maes are bonds issued by a government agency, the Federal National Mortgage Association (FNMA), which encourages home building by buying and selling mortgages to and from banks, savings and loan companies and real estate combines. When a bank, for instance, wants to liquidate some of its mortgages, it can sell them to the FNMA, which makes home financing more attractive to lending institutions. They have the advantage of producing occasionally comfortable yields and the plus factor of being easily liquidated in the market.

Compared to the tumult of a stock exchange floor, the bond market is fairly sedate. A typical bond firm in downtown Los Angeles has four salespeople who spend most of their time on the telephone, calling their accounts and advising them of new issues just placed on the market.

In one corner of the salesman's office is a loudspeaker hooked up to a direct phone line to the firm's New York office. A voice comes over the line announcing that their firm is one of a group that has made the successful low bid for a new bond issue from a Wisconsin utility company. That means the firm is one of several that will market the bonds to individual investors.

One salesman immediately gets on the phone to one of his customers, a Los Angeles bank that buys large amounts of bonds for its trust department. He tells the banker that the Wisconsin utility bond is available at 8.65 percent interest. Let's say he gets a turndown — the bank is interested only in larger issues.

Another salesman is on the phone to the trading desk of the firm's New York headquarters trying to obtain, for a client's benefit, the latest quotations on several bonds in the secondary market — that is, older bonds released from their original price restrictions and thus subject to fluctuations in the market.

It's a low-keyed business, dealing in bonds; no electronic tape recording of the latest price flutters on the Big Board bank in New York; not much excitement, because the traders do business mainly with banks, pension funds, and other conservative institutions. Hours pass before there's a stir of triumph in the room — one of the salesmen has sold 50 bonds of a new issue to the manager of a northern California retirement fund.

In this same area, but offering a little more excitement for the investor, is the *convertible debenture*. An ordinary debenture, like a bond, is a company's IOU. A convertible debenture differs in that it can be transformed into common stock issued by the company at a fixed price.

Say you've bought a debenture issued by National Electric for $1,000. It can be converted into 40 shares of common stock, which makes the conversion price $25 a share.

If National Electric's common stock rises to $36 a share, and you have the conversion privilege, converting the debenture gives you an $11 profit on each of your 40 shares. This happy turn of events, of course, would be reflected in the market value of National Electric's convertible debentures. And that's the beauty of buying such issues. If the company's common stock rises, you can profit through conversion. If it doesn't, you still have the interest coming in on the unconverted debenture — though if the common stock drops sharply, the market value of the issue will also be depreciated.

Bond prices simply don't move up and down as dramatically as stock market offerings. For those who like to operate aggressively in the money world, this is a quiet backwater. It's not to be ignored, however, if you want a safe shelter for your funds during a certain period. As Gerald Loeb points out, there is little point in buying bonds offering a low yield when "the cost of living has risen to such an extent that the total of interest and repaid principal in currency will buy only as much as or less than the principal itself at the time of the bond purchase." And *he* was writing back in the mid-thirties, when a movie cost a quarter and you could get a good meal for less than a dollar!

13

Real Estate: A Woman's Realm

If there is one area of investment for which a great many women have a special, built-in affinity, it is real estate. I suppose it goes back to our basic nest-building obsession. Early on, I seriously considered becoming a real estate broker like other women who have turned their concern for homebuilding and homemaking into something beyond emotional satisfaction. Some center their careers in real estate; others use it as their primary pattern of investment.

Property is capital. Real estate is basic, the oldest investment medium. And land has one unique characteristic that distinguishes it from other forms of investment. There is a limited supply of this commodity, which cannot be increased by any effort on man's part (other than such marginal operations as landfill or draining swamps). As Will Rogers said of land, "They ain't making it any more." Accordingly, as the population increases and the demand for land and property inevitably keeps pace, real estate prices can be expected to rise in the long run.

You may already have some experience in real estate dealing, especially if you own your own house. If so, you will have experienced one of the most important and appealing elements of real estate, which is referred to as "leverage." In real estate terms, leverage means the ability to control a sizable amount of property for a very small capital outlay. A more direct example of this fact is that most real estate can be purchased for a relatively small percentage of the overall cost of the property, generally in the 15 to 35 percent range. This, however, depends on how tight the money supply is. The balance of the purchase price is carried by a mortgage or trust deed held by a bank or some other lending institution. (A trust deed is an instrument by which legal title to real estate is conveyed to a third party to be held in trust for a lender until the debt secured by the instrument is paid. It is, in effect, a mortgage with three parties: the borrower, the lender and the trustee.)

Customarily these loans are repaid in equal monthly install-ments, often for 20 to 30 years, at a fixed interest rate. The fairly recent introduction of variable or adjustable-rate mortgages (ARMs) has revolutionized real estate financing. Interest rates on ARMs vary with the fluctuation of the cost of money—they're usually tied to T-bills or other indicators—and are adjusted annually or semi-annually. Their primary advantage over fixed-rate mortgages is that their rates, at least initially, are lower, making it easier for first time or lower income buyers to invest in property. This home-financing structure has enabled millions of Americans to own their own homes and produced one of the most phenomenal developments in the American economy. It also enlivens the possibilities for women interested in entering the real estate business.

Homeownership has a number of economic advantages in addition to the emotional satisfaction of establishing yourself on your own piece of dirt. In addition to leverage, the tax laws have been written to favor the homeowner in that all interest paid on the mortgage is tax-deductible. Since World War II, too, the value of such investments has in the majority of cases steadily risen (or appreciated) in value.

Richard Gibson, a real estate investment expert, cautions against "emotional involvement" when you venture into home-ownership. "The most important investment most people make in their lives is buying a house. And they make that investment from a purely emotional point of view. Many people buy houses that really aren't worth the purchase price because they buy them to keep 'forever.'

"This is a fallacy, because statistics show that the average house turns over once every eight years. There are exceptions to that, of course, but when you buy a house you should plan on how you're eventually going to get rid of it. You have got to think the thing completely through. You must say, 'Sure, everything is going to fall in place, and I am going to live in this house the next hundred years'—but what happens if something changes? What if I have to get rid of the house? Will I have so overimproved it that I'll lose a lot of money on it? Maybe the price you had to pay for your dream house was worth it to you. If so, be prepared to consider any loss the price you had to pay for a little extra enjoyment."

A woman buying a house on her own should be careful to lay down ground rules for herself. Spend no more than one-third of your annual income on the property—that is, on the monthly mortgage payments, taxes, insurance and maintenance. It is also advisable to set an absolute dollar limit in advance when shopping for a house or income property. If you start looking at a $135,000 house when you can realistically afford the payments only on a $95,000 house, you will only disappoint yourself from the very beginning and even be tempted to stretch your resources beyond the limits you can sensibly maintain.

Beware of minor but costly items as the "impound accounts" required by many home financing institutions. Such an account works like this: The bank requires that you pay the principal and interest on a monthly basis. But as taxes and insurance are paid on a semi-annual or annual basis, a lot of banks and lending institutions will require that you pay them an estimated amount to cover such payments. (They feel, somehow, that this provides assurance that you'll be able to meet your financial obligations. It's one way of protecting their interest in your investment.) The amount is placed in a non-interest bearing account. You forward your tax and insurance bill to the bank and they pay them out of your impound account.

Instead, I recommend that you set up an interest-bearing savings account in which you and the bank are joint proprietors, but from which you can't withdraw without their approval.

You'll run into some opposition from lenders on this issue, because financial institutions welcome opportunities to keep funds on deposit on which they don't have to pay interest. A surprising number of Americans have yet to take advantage of the new interest-bearing checking accounts; in essence, by keeping their funds in so-called "free" checking accounts, they are lending their hard-earned money to the banks interest free.

Homeownership has often led women down adventurous bypaths and into the volatile sphere of real estate investment. Success stories involving women and real property abound.

One of my favorites in this area is the story of how Pat Martin, whose real estate operations have boosted her into the $250,000 to $300,000 net-worth category, awakened to opportunity. Years ago, when she was responsible for the rearing of her two-year-old son, she had to go apartment-hunting.

"My son was with me," she recalls, "and the rental agent turned and said, 'Is that yours?' and I said, 'Yes, this young man is mine.' He said, 'We don't rent to children.' (Federal law now prohibits such discrimination, but income-property owners often find ways to get around the law.)

"This came as a rude awakening to me, that in looking for a

place to live, as basic a thing as can be, you are dependent on someone else, you're at their mercy. If you had a child or a dog in those days, you were entirely dependent on someone else's understanding attitude.

"And I made up my mind then that I would never in my life become dependent on anyone else for anything. So I determined that several things were necessary.

"First, we had to have a roof over our heads. I had a job at the time, but my income was barely enough to keep body and soul together, or so it seemed. Then I discovered that actually I had money to spend on other things, that I just had to rearrange my values a little."

Pat, who had come into a small inheritance, combined that with a small loan from her mother to make the down payment on an apartment building. "This assured me that I wouldn't be beholden to anyone else for anything so far as a roof over my head was concerned. We could have a go, we could do as we pleased because we owned the place. That put me in control. Then I could determine who was going to have the other apartments in the building, without restrictions on dogs or children. I was in the driver's seat for the first time in my life."

She began saving money from various sources and "eventually got to the point where I had enough money for other investments. In fact, when I made my first investment I didn't know how I was going to meet the obligations on the apartment building. But buying that property was my first real step toward independence."

Pat Martin also bought a house when she discovered she could meet all its obligations by renting it out. The rent covered the mortgage payment, utilities and taxes. As her monetary obligations on the house began to decrease, she found she had enough flexibility to buy a new car, and she was on her way to real estate operations on a much larger scale.

One of my favorite stories is that of Nancy Wagner, a California real estate broker in her mid-fifties. Twenty years ago, she inherited a small corner grocery store in Chicago, where she had grown up. Although its sale only netted her a few thousand dollars, she spent a portion of that money to hire a part-time sitter for her three small children and studied to get her real estate license. Even though she had barely made it through high school (having finished her courses at night after the birth of her first child), she knew she had an aptitude for the field.

She spent the remainder of her inheritance, six months later, on a down payment for a small California tract home, which had gone into foreclosure. In the face of much opposition from her husband who "didn't believe in real estate," she spent the commission from her first sale as a broker on a second property—a run-down duplex near the beach. Her goal then was to buy one piece of property a year. Even through "lean times" (her husband was often ill and out of work), she met that goal year after year.

Five years ago, she sold the duplex, which she had purchased for $26,000, for an astonishing $210,000 (a builder put up two condominiums on the lot). The little house in La Habra Heights, now a fashionable area, sold for $110,000. She had paid only $17,000 for it. Her real estate net worth is now in the millions, and many of the properties she has bought she has developed herself with assistance from her contractor son. She pays herself a "modest salary" each year from her commissions and spends the rest on property. She does, however, take a month off each year to "see the world she thought she'd only read about."

Needless to say, she is a firm believer that real estate is truly a "woman's realm." In spite of the fact that competition in the field is exceedingly stiff, she feels there is always room for the "street smart" woman with an aptitude for selling.

What's fascinating—and significant—about these two stories is that both women started out with very little in the way of capital and a great deal in the way of brains and energy.

Real estate may be your thing; this will be particularly true if you like the idea of working something visible and tangible, something less abstract than a stock certificate and less exhausting (in my opinion) than starting your own business.

As in other endeavors, it is absolutely necessary to educate yourself in the field. Burn that midnight oil. Read up on the subject, take a course in real estate management. Or, if you're well heeled, engage the services of a professional real estate analyst (not a broker). The field of real estate is complex; the legal aspects alone demand careful study. A professional approach is needed even if you *don't* intend to acquire a realtor's license and start up your own agency.

At the very least, you should consult an attorney specializing in real estate—one who has no financial interest in whether you buy or don't—before making any investment. If you are interested in getting an independent (not a lender's) appraisal on your property, contact a member of the Members Appraisal Institute (MAI), a professional organization similar in function and stature to that of CPAs. They belong to the American Institute of Real Estate Appraisers and can be contacted in cities throughout the United States. The MAIs are highly qualified individuals who are trained to appraise all types of property, from raw land to skyscrapers. Getting this type of appraisal is particularly valuable for tax and resale purposes; it also helps you to make sensible choices when you're deciding on a purchase.

If you go into real estate for investment purposes, you'll probably be interested mainly in income property; that is, structures that can be rented to people for homes or businesses, thus providing you with a regular monthly income. The purchase of "raw" land—undeveloped, usually remote from towns or cities, without water mains or electricity—is not generally advantageous, unless you can afford to have your money tied up for a time. There are several reasons for this. Chief among them is the fact that you have to pay for the land without receiving any "offsetting" income. Such land can suddenly become valuable, but it is a highly speculative investment and in recent years both individuals and some large companies have been badly burned. Raw land isn't worth much unless it is close to an expanding population center or is suitable for vacation or retirement homes.

The key to raw land is the price at which you buy it, the plan for improvement, and your financial staying power. In the early 1900s there was a substantial land offering on the East Coast advertised as beachfront property. The going price was around $20 an acre, on easy payment terms. Everything was going beautifully until one of the new landowners went down to view his property and found that it not only was ocean front, but was in fact swampland. The word got out, and the offering was soon hailed as a major land swindle. As the years went by, people sold the land at great loss in an effort simply to get rid of it. If you're wondering where this tale is leading, let me hasten to tell you that fifty years have passed and that same swampland is today called Miami Beach, where a front foot of highrise beach property can hardly be bought at *any* price. If you'd been an owner and had held that land over those fifty years, you would have multiplied your investment 1,000 times over.

A boarding-school teacher I know bought several acres of undeveloped land ten years ago in a then undeveloped area of southern California, about 50 miles south of Los Angeles. The area is now home to several small and medium-sized corporations and is fast becoming a financial center. That land is now worth six times what she paid for it — and there are very, very few Wall Street wizards who could match that rate of profit.

Another important point before you go into any real estate investment (in fact, *any* investment), is how you are going to get into it as well as out of it. By this I mean knowing how you're going to buy it, under what conditions, and how you will take title. And, most importantly, how you plan to dispose of it.

Let's take up the most common form of real estate investment, apartment houses.

Often the buyer of such income property will choose to

occupy one of the apartments herself, and that's not a bad idea — the closer watch you keep on your investment, the better. The success of such a venture depends on whether the return on the investment is as large as the investor expected it to be when she bought it. That return is, simply, the margin between total rental payments and the cost of owning and maintaining the apartment house.

An all-inclusive mathematical analysis of apartment-house operation is beyond the scope of this book, but here are a few principles that might serve as guidelines if your interest lies in this area. (Naturally you should supplement this by studying any of a number of books available on income property investment.)

One of the greatest hazards of such an operation, aside from having it located in a declining neighborhood, is a high vacancy rate. Before buying any such property you should check its rental records and determine the turnover in rentals — if rapid, why? — and question the tenants as to their satisfaction with their accommodations. In all cases you must assume a certain vacancy factor, usually at least five percent, as part of the normal state of things. If a real estate broker tries to tell you that the vacancies average much less than five percent, he or she is probably being less than truthful. Ask to see cash flow, rent receipts and operating expenses for the past two years.

In my interview with Pat Martin she estressed the importance of negotiating discounts on the many supplies and furnishings needed in operating an apartment house. Whittling down the dealer's markup on such items will often make a large difference in the profit of your operation.

Dealers are willing to go along with such discounts because of the prospective business, in volume, you'll presumably bring them. Or, as Pat Martin explained, "If you have ten apartments, you are going to buy ten refrigerators. You don't buy them all at once because they don't all have to be replaced at once. They are purchased at different times. Out of fifteen water heaters, for example, you might have eight to out in one year and the other seven over a period of years. If they come up with the right price this time, they might get invited to the dance the next time, and they know this. But you have to identify yourself in order to get the discount."

Another factor is the expense of maintenace, which depends in part on the age of the apartment house and the state in which it was previously maintained. Property always has to be maintained: walls painted, plumbing repaired, carpets replaced, wiring redone. And you should provide for such expenses beforehand, whether you manage the place yourself or have someone else do it. In addition to such expenses you should figure in your time, which could be devoted to some other profitable endeavor. You'll be occupied with paying for utilities, rubbish collection, landscape work, personal property taxes, real estate taxes – and this should all be figured as a cost factor.

The *cash flow* is the most important criterion of real estate management. This can be defined as the gross rentals, minus the vacancy factor, minus operating expenses, minus payments on the mortgage principal and interest. Your return is the annual cash flow divided by the down payment you made on the property. This figure normally should be about ten percent, based on realistic assumptions regarding the vacancy rate and the cost of maintenance.

If you succeed in finding income property that will provide you with a ten percent return on your investment, you will learn that with wise management, such an enterprise will have two considerable advantages:

As a tax shelter. In a typical apartment operation, the depreciation and interest payments are tax-deductible; a good part of the cash flow, if not all of it, will be tax-sheltered. This means, in turn, that your ten percent return on investment is roughly equal to the 15 to 20 percent you would have to earn on stock investments to gain the same after-tax effect. As always, the tax laws are quite complex and because the proposed tax bill could have a considerable effect on the tax-shelter aspect of income property, seek expert advice before making an investment.

As a hedge against inflation. It's a first-rate barrier against rising prices and cheaper money. If you're like most people who own and manage income property, a large part of your investment is borrowed money, repayable at a fixed rate over a determined number of years. Thus as the dollar gets cheaper, your payments will be made in dollars that have decreased in real value. This is in accordance with one of the maxims of inflation-fighting. Incur as much debt as possible (up to a certain point) and not, of course, personal debt, because the debt will be repaid with cheaper dollars.

To quote Richard Gibson: "You will find the predominance of wealth of the world can be traced to real estate. It's the safest investment you can make, provided it's carefully chosen. No matter how badly you get burned in a real estate deal, if you have staying power, inflation will eventually bail you out." Gibson believes that the primary reason for investing in real estate today is as a hedge against inflation; secondarily, to ensure that "at some point downstream that you have something to generate cash for your retirement years."

There is another hedging aspect to income-producing property: If inflation means you'll be able to raise your rents (unless you operate under rent control). Rents should increase at a faster rate than the growth of your operating expenses. Your cash flow and net income will rise. Those figures, in turn, will increase the value of your property when and if you decide to sell it.

Selling income property is usually advisable when depreciation no longer provides a shelter for your income. Some of the gain or appreciation (the difference between what you sold the property for and what you paid for it) will be subject to long-term capital gains treatment, which means that the taxes should be substantially lower than on ordinary income. Without going into all the technicalities of the very complex tax law in this area, you will generally receive favorable tax treatment on your real estate holdings from the tax-shelter aspect while you are holding it and the partial long-term capital gains treatment when you sell it.

But there is a negative side, too. Often it's difficult to locate an apartment house or other income-producing property on which a small investor can afford the down payment. In such cases you may well find it necessary to join forces with a friend or associate to swing the deal.

If you're in the financially undernourished category, you might want to consider "fix-up property." That is, you buy a house or apartment building in run-down condition, at a modest price and renovate it. But be warned: *Never* buy run-down property in a deteriorating neighborhood. No matter how beautifully you renovate it, its value will rarely increase above the value of neighboring properties and will *definitely* decrease when other area properties decline in value. Many people have bought such property in a desirable neighborhood and managed to resell at a handsome profit after earning income during the period of ownership.

Before investing in any apartment complex, whatever its size, make certain that you've considered the following factors:

• Structural soundness. Always have an independent contractor, engineer or architect thoroughly inspect the property, and ask for a written evaluation of the quality of construction and structural soundness.

• Management. If it's a small property—two to ten units—you'll probably want to manage it yourself, if it's located within 30 miles of your home. If the project is large, make sure that the current management team is qualified; if the property is not managed by an on-site team, the company should be located near the project and should be familiar with the neighborhood.

• Location. Make sure that the area is not overbuilt with competing projects; you'll have problems controlling the vacancy rate if this is the case. Obviously, you want the best location you can afford, but it isn't imperative that you buy into the "high rent" district to get a good return on your investment.

• Operating expenses. Whenever possible, these costs should be imposed on tenants, especially if required repairs result from carelessness on the part of the tenants. Try to keep these costs at a minimum, by taking advantage of dealer discounts, "warehouse" and "seconds" appliance sales, and by buying in bulk supplies you know you'll need on a continuing basis.

• Stability/Quality of tenants. The most stable tenants are usually families (they're less transient), and older persons in high income brackets.

• Seller responsibilities. In many cases, the seller should have continuing responsibilities beyond the sale of the property. Especially if the project is new, get a contract in writing by which you're protected against structural defects and, possibly (if the seller has made distinct claims regarding expected income) against operating deficits.

• Seller's projections. Carefully evaluate for feasibility and correctness, a seller's claims relating to rents, operating expenses and cash return. It is advisable to do a market study of other properties in the area, getting as much information as possible, to determine whether the seller's claims are credible.

• Financing. In order to receive a balanced return from cash flow, tax benefits and equity buildup, your mortgage financing should cover approximately 75 percent of the purchase price.

• Suitability for condominium conversion. As property becomes more expensive, many Americans who want to invest in real estate are opting for condos and coops. If your project can be converted to condominums without astronomical expense, you could have a source of substantial profit. This is just one possibility to consider, though, and shouldn't be your primary reason for investing in a particular project.

Industrial/Commercial Income Property

The other type of income property is industrial and commercial. Such property is often expensive, an impossible area for the small investor unless she pools her resources with those of other people.

Commercial and industrial property can provide a strong and steady source of income. All-important is the quality of tenant to whom you lease the property. Ideally, the tenant should have an excellent (and verifiable) credit rating and the lease should be on a net-net-net basis. This means that the tenant, not the owner, pays for all expenses attendant to the property including taxes, repairs, maintenance and upkeep; in short, everything except the mortgage payment. The risk is low and the precalculated return on the investment may be greater than that of other forms of real estate operation. It also lends itself to absentee ownership.

For these reasons, mortgage loans can be made on commercial/industrial property, particularly if the tenant is a good credit risk. A long-term lease can have the same inflation-hedging and appreciation advantages that apartment houses often do, particularly by providing in the long-term lease that the annual rental is increased in direct ratio with the Cost of Living Index or some other fairly accurate economic indicator such as the GNP Deflator (Gross National Product Deflator).

Now for the negative side of commercial/industrial property. One is that the improvements or structural changes made by the lessee will tend to be single-purpose. Suppose you lease your building to a fast-food chain or a similar franchise operation. You would have great difficulty in releasing the property without making expensive alterations to the interior and exterior of the structure. A less dramatic example might be a tenant engaged in industrial manufacturing who would want improvements on the building—improvements that might be of no value to the tenant who succeeds him. This is the great drawback to industrial/commercial property ownership. Being aware of that, you should demand of your first tenant a commensurate return on the risk you take or require the tenant to make the changes himself and leave them in place when he gives up the lease. This clause is usually included in such leases.

If you have, say, a 10,000-square-foot building for assembly or light industry of some kind, it will often attract entrepreneurs without much capital or a high credit rating. Here you're taking the risk that they will fail before the expiration of the lease and leave you with the problem of a long vacancy during which you try to find another tenant. A safer investment, probably, is the recently popular mini-warehouse in which you rent space to householders for possessions they can't find room for in their homes or garages.

Location is all-important in any real estate development. Whether it's an apartment house or industrial/commercial property, you should consider such paramount factors as the accessibility of public transportation, the declining or advancing status of the district, the incidence of crime in the neighborhood, the availability of housing nearby if it's an industrial building. You also must have staying power, which means you should have calculated your financial position carefully enough so that you can be sure you'll be able to keep up the mortgage payments even in periods of adversity, to survive even if you run into an increased vacancy rate. If you have enough capital or income to get over the rough spots, you'll find that time often favors the investor who is farsighted enough to hang on to his property, gradually improve it, and profit from the long-run upward trend of real estate values.

Another important factor is knowing how to negotiate (and not being diffident about doing so). We'll cover this in detail in Chapter 15, so I won't belabor it here. You can be sure that people with real estate to sell will be asking quite a bit more than they really expect to get. If you pay the asking price without at least trying for a lower price, you are lacking in common sense, or at least common knowledge. Pat Martin cites the case of a "very unsophisticated couple" who several years ago were interested in a house for which the asking price was $47,000. "They did not know that it was customary to negotiate or that they should have offered $40,000 to $42,500 to induce the sellers to come down to around $45,000. So their inability to negotiate cost them at least several thousand dollars. Nobody has ever come along and handed me that much money for nothing."

Shopping For Mortgages

Believe it or not, shopping for a loan is much like shopping for any other large purchase. If you're working with a broker, chances are he or she has certain lenders – or connections – in the mortgage business. But that doesn't mean that you have to follow your broker's advice in choosing a loan or a lender; as with any investment, doing your homework is essential. Keep in mind that bigger is not necessarily better, and that there are other options for obtaining loans than the commercial lending institutions.

Obviously, whether you opt for a fixed-rate or variable-rate loan, you want to get the lowest intrate you can find. Despite stiff competition among lenders, rates *do* vary somewhat. In the first few years of the life of your loan, the bulk of your payments goes toward interest. Which is why, especially if you anticipate keeping the property for a short time, it makes sense to find a low rate. The greatest variation in rates you will find will be among the variables. In some cases, the spread may be as great as one percentage point; difference in annual payments between, say, a nine percent or ten percent, $100,000 loan can be substantial.

Interest rates, though vitally important, are only one factor to consider in evaluating different loan packages. Often a lower interest rate is offset by other conditions, such as a stiff pre-payment penalties or negative amortization (you pay less interest initially but make up the difference between that rate and the "going" interest rate later in the life of the loan).

Points, the fee the lender charges you for making the loan, are equal to one percent of the mortgage amount. You pay points at the time you obtain the loan. These can vary widely, from a low of one point to a high of around 2.5 points. Again, a lower interest rate may be offset by a higher points charge, so be sure to read the fine print. This fee may, in some cases, be tax deductible, meaning that depending on your tax situation and the length of time you anticipate holding the property, it may be in your interest to pay more points for a lower interest rate.

Pre-payment privileges are a must. Even if you have to pay a fee to exercise this right, make sure that your loan allows for it. Another consideration is whether the loan is "assumable," which means basically that your bank agrees in advance that a buyer can take over your mortgage. This will enable you to sell your property more quickly, especially when interest rates are high. When rates are low, it will be more difficult to find lenders making assumable loans, since they stand to lose a substantial amount if they allow your buyer to take over your ten percent loan when the going rate is twelve percent.

A balloon payment, a fixed lump sum or balance of principal due the lender at a specified time (usually at maturity of the mortgage), is becoming less common at this writing. It's probably best to avoid making a loan with such a clause, unless you feel certain that your financial circumstances or expected appreciation of your property will allow you to make a large payment when the loan matures.

Loan maturities typically range from 15 to 30 years, although in recent years I have heard that some lenders are making 40-year mortgages. The longer the maturity, the lower the payments and the higher the total interest paid over the life of the loan. If your income is low, you'll want the longest maturity you can get; if you're approaching retirement and can afford larger payments, you might opt for a loan with a shorter maturity, providing you with a more rapid build-up of equity and a lower total interest charge.

Alternative Mortgage Instruments

Depending on your situation, you may want to consider some of the alternatives to the conventional mortgage. We've already discussed the adjustables, the most common of these, but there are others.

Rollover mortgages have an initial term of three, four or five years, and can be renewed (at the option of the lender) for up to five additional periods.

A graduated-payment mortgage allows you to keep your payments low in the first few years of the loan. Later in the loan, however, payments will be larger than those you might have made on a conventional loan, to make up for the interest loss in the early years. This option may be suitable for someone who could not purchase property otherwise, for instance, someone in the early years of a career that promises a substantial increase in income later on.

In *shared-appreciation mortgages*, a lender agrees to give the borrower below-market rate of interest in return for a share of the appreciation in a borrower's property over a specified period of time (usually ten years).

In *growth-equity mortgages*, payments in the first years are the same as for conventional mortgages; each year after, the payments grow progressively larger. The increases are applied to the principal of the loan, allowing a borrower to pay off a 30-year maturity loan in, say, 13 to 15 years.

Second mortgages aren't actually variations on conventional mortgages but additional, or, as the name implies, secondary loans. If you cannot come up with all of the down payment, you might find a lender—perhaps even the property's seller—to loan you to additional amount. The holder of the first mortgage has the largest claim to your property, should you default on your loan; the holder of the second mortgage would be next in line. For this reason, second mortgages usually command higher than market rates of interest.

I have mentioned the above options not so much because I recommend them, but rather because in today's real estate market—a volatile and high-priced one—traditional mortgages often cannot adequately cover all situations. Perhaps it all sounds rather complicated, and it can be, but it shouldn't deter the venturesome woman from pursuing a promising investment in real estate.

Reit's and Real Estate Limited Partnerships

Whether you have $5000 or $50,000 to invest in real estate, you may want to consider yet another shared ownership option—the real estate investment trust (REIT). In these trusts or partnerships, public and private, an investment firm pools the funds of a group of investors, your share, or fractionalized interest, is treated legally as if it were a security, just like a share of stock in a corporation. REIT's are heavily regulated by federal and state law, and a prospectus is issued to potential investors. Chances are you'll never meet any of your co-investors, even though you jointly participate in the ownership of the property, which is usually a commercial or a large-scale residential apartment project.

The limited partnership, one which has fewer than 35 investors, all of whom meet certain income and financial criteria, is basically exempt from many of the cumbersome securities laws and regulations. The limited partnership is usually formed to purchase one property, such as a suburban shopping center. This type of joint ownership can be profitable, but it is essential that you seek a competent financial advisor or attorney to evaluate the investment if you're venturing into unknown waters.

14
*The Tax Man Cometh**

It's only fitting that I should devote a chapter to that sometimes menacing bureaucracy, the Internal Revenue Service. A fact of life, taxes have to be lived with, and understood. Coping successfully with them can often mean the difference between profit and loss on your year's operations. And they have to be dealt with on a continuing basis, not just as something to be fretted over the night of April 14. The tax laws are constantly being changed by Congress and the revisions must be noted and, if possible, taken advantage of *as they are made.* Many people discover they've been too generous to Uncle Sam when it's too late.

You can keep up with the ebb and flow of tax legislation through a number of softcover books such as the *Prentice-Hall Federal Tax Handbook* and the *J.K. Lasser Tax Institute*, which are issued annually in new editions. They will provide specific ways of obtaining legal tax savings as well as defining areas where

*At this writing, a new tax bill is in the works which will, if passed, affect much of the material in this chapter. I suggest that you check with your tax attorney or refer to either of the books mentioned above for the latest tax treatment information.

deductions cannot be taken. You should also read and thoroughly understand the brochure the government sends you with its income tax forms. If it is unclear, don't gloss over it. What you don't understand can cost you money. One place to get help (not the best, in my opinion, but the cheapest) is the IRS, which provides a service on a year-round basis in order to answer your questions. Of course, the closer you get to tax time, the more waiting time is involved in getting information from these offices.

Every year you should take it for granted that the federal tax code resembles that designation "terra incognita" found on some maps, unmapped territory bristling with swamps and quicksand.

Here are a number of brief suggestions regarding income taxes that should be emblazoned in your mind when you sit down to the annual tussle with your conscience, your sense of discretion, and your IRS return.

Don't ever cheat. I underline this admonition because the money you might save simply isn't worth the sleepless nights it entails or the chance you'll be caught in an audit, with heavy penalties to pay. Besides, it would be wrong.

Remember: *There is no statute of limitations on tax fraud.* And a fraudulent return is *your fault* — not that of the person who may have filled out your return.

Having made this point, let me now advise you: Don't be afraid to use every *legitimate* means of lowering your tax within the rules of the tax code. Be aware of the difference between legal *avoidance* and illegal *evasion.* On judgmental issues it is perfectly permissible to give yourself a break — and then pay up if an IRS agent disagrees.

If you're in the 30 percent-plus tax bracket, you should have your returns made out by a tax accountant. Generally, he or she will save you more — sometimes much more — than the fee involved in retaining an accountant.

It's a fact that income taxes become a thorny problem just when your income rises to the level at which you can consider investing whatever savings or capital you've accumulated.

If you are self-employed, you should, if circumstances dictate, take advantage of HR-10, the so-called Keogh plan. This provides, through an act passed by Congress in 1963, for your own retirement fund. Under a recent amendment to the act's provisions, you can set aside the lesser of twenty-five percent or $30,000.00 of your annual income. This amount is deductible from your income tax. Also the tax on any dividends or capital gains or interest received from HR-10 may be deferred while you're accumulating the fund. Keogh investments may be made in open-end mutual funds, annuities, endowment or life insurance contracts, savings and loan certificates, or a series of U.S. bonds authorized for this purpose. And, as of this writing, your IRA contribution is not taxed.

The most important thing about handling your tax liability, which gets bigger and more complex as your wealth increases, is to realize that it can't be deferred until a few days before the deadline. You have to plan, to plot your course ahead of time. You should start tax planning in December for the following year — *16 months* in advance of payment.

If you keep up to date on how much tax you're incurring on your income, you can save yourself money. Then you can take advantage of the fluctuations. For instance, you might cash in your government "EE" bonds in a low-income year. These bonds are taxable in the year cashed or the taxpayer may elect to report the taxable increments for each year as income for that year.

All this is part of your essential record-keeping. You should maintain a running account of your earnings and return on your investments. You should keep copies of everything you send the IRS. It's equally essential to retain all cancelled checks. In general, records should be kept for six years after the tax return was or should have been filed, whichever is later.

You must also master the basics of the tax system. For better or worse, they're an integral part of your life; they won't just go away so long as you are producing enough income to be taxed. The whole subject becomes less scary the more you know about it. There are certain angles you should know about. That, for instance, you can be penalized if you under-estimate your income (as a self-employed person) by ten percent or more. That it's vital to file an *amended return* if you discover that, knowingly or not, you've cheated the government out of its share. Probably your best safeguard against slipping into trouble with Uncle Sam (next to becoming an expert in the subject as possible) is to have the advice of a good tax accountant on a continuing basis—not merely to fill out your returns but to consult on the best moves to make during the year that will enable you to take full advantage of any possible tax breaks.

For those who have started a business on their own or initiated an investment program, there are several areas that must be thoroughly understood.

The first principle is that you should never make an investment decision for tax reasons alone. The two must be kept separate. If a certain stock has appreciated greatly in value since you bought it, don't make the mistake of not taking your profit because you don't want to pay the capital gains tax. This is foolish. As an example, if the stock you bought for $20 three years ago is now selling for $75 and you have no reason to believe it will go higher, sell it and pay for your long-term capital gain of $55. If your tax amounts to $11 (the approximate tax if your normal income tax bracket is 50 percent percent), be glad you made your after-tax profit of $44 per share.

Capital Gains and Losses

There are important distinctions in the types of gains and losses. A *long-term capital gain* is incurred if you buy securities or real estate and hold them for more than six months before selling them. On this type of transaction you are subject to only forty percent of the regular tax rates on income.

A *short-term capital gain* is one resulting from holding a stock or bond or any kind of property six months or less. You pay the regular tax rate — the same as on any other kind of income — on a short-term gain. Therefore it possesses no tax advantage.

You should keep a careful running account of purchases or sales of stocks or bonds, noting whether there are long-term or short-term gains involved. And keep equally careful records of sales and purchase dates, especially the confirmation slips issued by brokerages which establish the exact dates on the transactions. It's the kind of thing an IRS auditor might demand to see. The Lasser guide I mentioned earlier covers the tax implications of investments in a solid, straightforward manner.

Managing Your Income Taxes

The best thing any taxpayer can do is to keep good records. This means that you *must* know where your money came from and where it went during the year. Get organized and write down everything that happens to you financially. At the end of the year when you meet your tax preparer, you should have everything at your fingertips, even items or expenses which may not be deductible (it's definitely better to have too much than to forget a deduction to which you may be entitled). And the key to making the most of your deductions is to keep accurate and detailed records. Keep your cancelled checks, your cash receipts (too often cash purchases are forgotten — and they can add up to a significant amount). Keep a log of your auto mileage: the business portion, commuting miles and even personal mileage. Save all of those printouts from American Express, Visa, MasterCard and any other charge cards — there are probably business related expenses in there, not to mention the interest charges.

Following is a basic checklist of items to include in your payment records (and don't forget the charge card purchases —

even though they haven't been paid for in the current year). For tax purposes the IRS considers them paid for!

Interest. All interest, such as for home mortgage payments, revolving charge accounts, auto loans, personal loans, and even interest paid to the IRS.

Taxes. Real and personal property taxes paid to state and local governments, license fees for your cars, general sales tax on all the small items you bought during the year plus sales tax on large purchases such as cars or boats.

Contributions. Do you drop $25 a week into the collection basket at your church? Or did you donate to the Salvation Army? (Be sure to get a receipt from them when the garage sale leftovers are picked up). For large donations of appreciated property such as heirlooms or paintings, get some advice from your tax advisor. Have you bought raffle tickets, attended the sheriff's rodeo, or given a couple of dollars at the door or on the street? It all adds up rather quickly at the end of the year. Did you have a payroll deduction for charity? Think about it and write everything down for your tax preparer.

Medical. You actually have to have incurred substantial expenses to get in on these, but there are some expenses other than regular medical and dental bills which may take you over the standard deduction threshold. These may include nursing services, glasses, psychiatric counseling or costs for substance abuse treatment centers, and all of the mileage you incurred in getting to the doctor's office.

Beyond the basics, there are some little known, miscellaneous deductions not widely publicized by the IRS. Among the ones that most people either don't remember or don't know about are:

- •Union dues and fines
- •Tax preparation fees from last year
- •Memberships (for the self-employed or outside salespeople) or other unreimbursed expenses you may run up
  in promoting your business

- Telephone expenses (business related)
- Personal computers and software
- Business periodical subscriptions; securities custodian fees
- Mortgage points
- Moving expenses (if new employment has taken you over 35 miles from your former home); this includes all the regular moving costs, house hunting trips, meals and lodging, home sale expenses, etc.
- Educational courses and expenses (such as books and other materials) taken to improve your job skills or your investment acumen
- Home office expenses (these are being closely watched by the IRS, so it's best to consult with your tax preparer before you get too involved)
- Job-hunting expenses. If you looked for a job in the same business or trade this year, the costs of your resume, phone calls, agency fees, travel to interviews, meals and lodging (among others) are deductible.
- Casualty losses. These are subject to some limitations, after which you may deduct losses of your personal property and the deductible amount on car damages, burglaries, fires, etc.
- Child care credits. Even some summer camp expenses can be included here, but there is a limitation for the total expense based on your income.

Business Taxes

If you think recordkeeping for your personal taxes is a chore, wait until you get to your business records! (I should know, having started a half a dozen or so companies in the last 20 years.) It's advisable, if you can afford it, to secure the services of a reliable bookkeeper, who will remind you monthly or quarterly to keep your act together. It's *essential* to have a tax advisor and an together. It's *essential* to have a tax advisor and an attorney.

There are some basics to consider here, and these apply especially to those who may still be employed but are itching to get out on their own. Consult with your tax advisor *before* deciding on your business structure. The options are corporations, sub-chapter S corporations, partnerships, limited partnerships or sole proprietorships. Your tax advisor can help you determine which is the best course based on the type of business you're starting, your personal income tax situation and other factors. The tax implications of the various business structures vary widely, and each has its benefits and disadvantages. It's not a decision to be taken lightly, as it can affect your personal income tax situation, and even your personal assets, for years to come.

Deductions for Investors

If you have any sort of investment program going, you can probably claim deductions from your federal income tax on a number of items you may not have considered. Singly they may seem a drop in the bucket, but added together they can result in substantial savings.

You may deduct for investment counseling, for renting the safety deposit box in which your stock certificates are kept, for the expenses of getting to and from your broker's office, for the services of an accountant who handles your investments; you may legitimately claim subscriptions to periodicals and newsletters, any transfer taxes you might pay the state on stock transactions, preparation of your income tax return, and any expenses (telephone, stamps, office supplies) incurred in managing your investments.

Types of Returns

Whether you itemize or take standard deductions is something you should decide after figuring it out both ways. Naturally you take the one that will cost you the least.

Usually, if you're married, you'll get a better break by filing a joint return. In some cases, however, it is advantageous to file separate returns. The only way you can find out, though, is by figuring it both ways and adopting the least expensive course.

Audits

How do audits come about? How do you respond if your taxes are audited? Contrary to current legend, there is no malignant gnome somewhere spinning a roulette wheel lined with all our names. The Internal Revenue Service runs all returns through its computers, and each area of the return is keyed to a percentage of your total income, particularly tax shelter losses. Your return *may* then be pulled for a closer secrutiny by an agent of the IRS. If that bureau should decide there may be grounds for an audit, they set up a meeting, either at their local office or at your office or home. (The locale of the meeting is usually determined by where and how voluminous your records are. If the audit is routine, you will probably have to go to the IRS office.)

How should you act? No tricks, slights, or evasive ploys apply here. Your attitude should be one of full and open cooperation, but not obsequiousness or timidity (unless, of course, you have something to feel guilty about; in which case, my condolences). But if by any chance the agent should prove aggressive or hostile, *don't* try to play his game. Simply break off the meeting and ask to speak with his supervisor; and it might be a good idea to bring someone along with you to the next meeting.

Should you bring a lawyer or your tax person to the first meeting? Probably not, unless you know up front you're going to need one. If you do, don't waste time. Wheel in your professionals at the opening bell and get right down to cases.

In that first meeting, let *them* ask the questions. If you don't have the exact answers to some, don't wing it. Look up the information, or if you can't do that then and there, ask for another meeting.

How often does the IRS collect? Well, how often do police officers give tickets? While the IRS *claims* they're not on a quota system, the statistics are grim: eight times out of ten they dig out something that will cost you. You don't have to accept their decision, though; if you've got solid grounds for disagreeing with the agent, you can ask to speak with his or her supervisor. If the matter is still unresolved, your next option is the Appellate Division, which serves as an intermediary between the IRS and the Federal Tax Court. These higher levels of appeal naturally become costly but in some cases they may be worth the effort.

All returns that are called are not necessarily audited. The number of audits also depends on how busy the IRS happens to be. If they have time on their hands, they do lots of audits; if they're swamped, they have to let a lot of returns slip by. (I wouldn't advise fudging on your return on the chance they might be overworked that week.)

Gifts and Estate Taxes

Anyone with family responsibilities — and indeed any responsible person — will want to consider these matters.

The federal tax code permits anyone to give $10,000 in cash or stocks or other property each year to any number of people without paying any gift tax on it. Nor do the recipients have to pay income tax on the gifts. Thus if you had four children, you could give each of them $10,000 a year every year. If your husband joins in the project, he too can give $10,000 tax-free to any number of individuals.

Thus it is possible for you to give away a sizable portion of your estate without incurring a tax liability. It's a good way to provide for your children's education for instance, by giving them the money *before* they are ready for college, investing it meanwhile in securities or whatever you choose.

As any probate expert will tell you, estate taxes, which must be paid within nine months after death and after other debts and attorneys' fees have been taken care of, can be very high and escalate rapidly if the estate is valued at more than $500,000. For 1987 and thereafter, that figure is $600,000.

"The power to tax involves the power to destroy," the great Chief Justice Marshall observed in a famous decision — to which a lot of us could murmur, "Amen." Taxes are a continuing burden, and a heavy one, but if you gain an understanding of the system and move within it adroitly, you won't be destroyed. And there's also gratification in feeling yourself to be a productive member of society. Wisely handled, your tax problems can be kept under control — *your* control — and you'll have enough after-tax income to achieve financial independence. *Anticipation* is the watchword here, along with hard-won expertise.

Estate Planning

If you have been successful or hope to be successful in your investment career, you should consider what to do about your eventual estate. This is especially important if you have the sole responsibility for your children. The bottom line in estate planning is minimizing the inheritance and estate taxes and conserving your assets for those you care about.

In most states you pay a state inheritance tax as well as the federal estate tax. According to Nancy Boxley Tepper, a California estate attorney, "You have various deductions that you can take. Funeral expenses, the costs of the last illness, etc. What is left, the next estate, is taxed at a pretty hefty rate. All this is part of planning your financial future. Good planning will result in your children or other beneficiaries receiving as much as possible of what you've built up from a lifetime of effort."

Living revocable trusts are an excellent way of guaranteeing such results. Basically, a trust is an instrument under which legal title is held by one party, the trustee, for the benefit of other parties. A bank holds assets as trustee for other parties. Or an individual can act as trustee for other parties or for himself or herself.

One of the main advantages of a living recoverable trust is that the property isn't subject to probate when the person who established the trust dies. If an estate is subject to probate, a year or more may pass before the estate is distributed — and there will be statutorily fixed attorneys' fees, executor's commissions and court costs.

As Ms. Tepper says, "younger women with small children should consider two factors. First, the appointment of a reliable person as their guardian; second, the creation of a trust that will protect their future, since you wouldn't be leaving your holdings to them outright. You should spell out very carefully at what ages you want the children to receive their shares in your estate, taking into consideration college and medical expenses. If it is a small estate, you may want the remaining funds distributed to the children when they reach twenty-one. If larger, you will probably want it distributed at intervals."

The cornerstone of estate planning is your will. For without one, the state where you legally reside will make all decisions on your estate, how it is to be transferred, taxed, and distributed. There is simply no substitute for a will. Perhaps the best advice I can give you is not to attempt to make one up yourself. Turn the problem over to an attorney. The fees for drawing up a will are relatively standard and the complexity of a will varies with the size and complexity of your estate. When discussing your will with an attorney you will need to make the following decisions: Who will your beneficiaries be? You will need to make a list of the various people, whether members of your family or associates or friends, to whom you wish portions of your estate transferred.

The next step is to decide what you're going to have transferred. Perhaps the best way to go about this is to use your net worth calculation, which you developed in Chapter 3. It is very important to be thorough in this area and include everything you legally own from stocks, bonds, and real estate to furs, jewelry, and other personal items. You will also want to consider such areas as royalties due you, ownership in companies — whatever. You'll need to determine who the executor of your estate will be and, if you choose, you may decide to have joint executors such as your husband and your child. If it's a particularly complex estate, you might also want to consider specifying an attorney or business associate as executor. Another consideration will be the guardians for your children.

Perhaps one of the most important elements of a will is that it needs to be reviewed periodically and changed along with any major changes in your life. Wills should also be amended whenever a major property in your will is sold or a new one acquired. Some changes may necessitate the drawing up of an entirely new will. In other circumstances your will may require only a codicil (an amendment). However, it's important to remember that a codicil needs to be both witnessed and legally drawn. If a codicil is added to a will and either not witnessed or not signed or in some other way improperly drawn, it can invalidate your entire existing will. The making of a will is often thought of as something to be done later on in life, but I believe that no matter what age you are, you should have a will if only out of consideration for those you care about.

15
How To Get Your Own Way: The Art of Negotiation

Negotiation touches every aspect of your life. It's a process we're all involved in—on a daily basis—whether we realize it or not. From its most subtle manifestations, the way you fill out a loan application or dress for a meeting with your banker, to its most extreme, sitting across the table from potential investors who've been asked to contribute $50,000 to your business venture, negotiating is a fact of life for the woman who wants to get ahead.

Forget about those antiquated notions that negotiating is demeaning—that a woman "with character" doesn't haggle. Since the earliest days, bargaining has been an integral part of American business tradition. Whether you're signing a lease, trying to get a bank loan, buying or selling your house or car, or seeking a new job or a raise, you're going to have to negotiate.Negotiating is, quite simply, the only way to make the most of your opportunities. And unless you're prepared to haggle with, browbeat and out-maneuver the best of them, chances are you won't get what you want—or need.

In a "60 Minutes" interview, Morley Safer asked Bobby Knight, Indiana University's basketball coach, what he considered the most essential factor in his team's success. Knight's response was simple and direct. "The courage to prepare," he replied.

Courage and preparation are the keystones to success in most of life's ventures—and they're absolutely essential in successful negotiation. You *must* do your homework, and that entails drawing up a precise blueprint of what you hope to achieve, and being acutely aware of what you will accept as an absolute minimum.

In this chapter, you will learn how to prepare for every negotiation involving money; the basic guidelines of every negotiation; how to cope with fear and anxiety; and what *not* to do when you're negotiating. Keep in mind that not all strategies will make you feel comfortable. You'll have to tailor your negotiating style to suit your own personality and motivations. Also remember that some deals are right—for both parties—from the very beginning, and require no negotiation.

Commit to memory (and, preferably, to paper) your needs and objectives, alternative offers and fallback positions, as well as what you *must* gain and what you can reasonably concede. These facts, and your command of them, are vital; the more established they are in your mind, the greater ease and manner of presentation you'll bring to the negotiating table.

Bargaining, from the days of the horse traders and peddlers, is ingrained in the American business tradition. Few of us realize this. To some American women, however, there is something repugnant or demeaning about haggling. It's something she thinks happens only in the souks of Middle Eastern cities. The result, of course, is that the American woman traveler is usually regarded abroad as a prime sucker.

Perhaps negotiating can best be characterized by the famous words from the Sermon on the Mount: "Ask and you shall receive."

Most of us negotiate every day of our lives. But not all of us are aware that we're negotiating. It's just silly to ignore this fact. If you are being interviewed for a new job you may be able to secure as much as $2,500 a year more, simply by using sound negotiating techniques and holding your ground at the crunch.

Let's begin with that most common (and vexing) situation: asking the boss for a raise. It's no secret that a lot—an awful lot—of women are doing jobs worth a good deal more than they're getting paid for. The issue is learning how to get paid what you're worth. I've been on both sides of this barrier, both as employer and as employee. It was only after I became an employer that I realized what chances I'd passed up as an employee—how strong my essential position had been and how foolishly I'd failed to take advantage of it.

So here you are. You want a raise, and your employer has to be convinced that you deserve one. One of the basic planks in negotiation is casting a cool eye on the overall picture: You must establish your own position first. Begin by asking yourself these questions:

1. How valuable am I to the firm?
2. What would it cost in time and money to replace me and train someone else?
3. What is the worst that could happen if my employer said no?
4. Can I get a job somewhere else? How easily? Do I have contacts in othr firms in the same field?
5. Does my company or department have the available funds to grant a raise?
6. Are others in my company being paid more than I am for the same job? Am I performing more than one job?
7. What is my relationship to my boss?
8. What have I done for my employer or company lately (cut costs, increased production, raised sales, whatever)?

After you've asked yourself these questions and have come up with good answers to them, you're ready to develop your game plan:

1. Try to make your presentation to your boss outside his office. If possible, invite him to lunch or meet him in your office or the conference room. This breaks the chief-subordinate pattern and can lighten the psychological pressure on you.

2. Have your reasons for a raise carefully defined. If you don't feel comfortable saying them out loud, write them down and hand them to him during the meeting. But it's much better to talk it out — the spoken word is usually softer and more pliable that the written one.

3. Determine exactly how large a raise you want and how much it would cost the company by the hour, month and year. This is important. You must know precisely what you're talking about. Then ask for slightly more than you expect, in order to leave room for negotiating.

4. Be sure *you*, not your boss, suggest the amount of the increase.

There are a number of tactics that have been used very effectively (on me, I might add) within this framework. One, of course, is the power play of telling your employer you've received an offer for a similar position with another company, for more money. This can give you excellent leverage — unless, of course, it makes him so made he gives you your walking papers. This last point is one you must weigh very carefully before your meeting.

The other approach — not recommended, just mentioned in passing — is the third-party negotiating method. This is where you let it be known through your boss's secretary or some other key employee that you've had another offer and you "don't know what to do about it." Be sure to tell your intermediary the subject is confidential. If he or she is a good, loyal type, and you yourself are a valued employee, the word will get out, and you'll get your raise, for one reason: The boss won't want to lose you.

Another tip: Don't let resentment at being passed over make you so angry that you defeat your own purpose. In any firm, but especially in a fledgling one, it's possible that your boss is simply too busy or too harried to remember when it's salary review time for you. He or she may even be waiting to be reminded. Executives often like to see signs of aggressive spirit, a sense of inherent worth, in their subordinates. My very capable assistant at Infonics, Inc., Barbara Hauser, used to give me a gentle reminder at review time. There was never any question in my mind that she was due for a raise, but I was working my head off at the time or away in the field, and if she hadn't reminded me, she might have gone for several months without her due increase.

Obviously, these suggestions are designed to give you leverage, but they should be used only if you've been a "good and faithful servant." If you haven't, you could end up being embarrassed — and unemployed. Be sure your self-analysis is carefully and accurately thought out.

Now let's talk about negotiating in general. The main principles involved in the art of negotiation (aside from the realization that if you don't get your way, or as much of it as is reasonable, the other fellow will get his and you'll be sorry) apply to many situations:

1. Establish credibility as your first move. Make the other person realize that you are aboveboard, trying to be constructive rather than trying to take unfair advantage. Impress the other party with your straightforwardness and honesty. Don't be too tough or drive too hard a bargain, at least in the beginning; no one wants to work with a "sharp operator."

2. Always try to hold the negotiating session on your turf — your office or your home, or, second best, on neutral territory such as a restaurant. You won't always have a choice of sites, but when you do, take it.

3. Get concessions from the other as early as possible. For example, if you're negotiating for a lease, ask the lessor for fresh

paint in the living room or new storm sashes — anything, however small, that might induce him to make a concession. It will set a precedent for the meeting. Ease him into the habit of saying "yes" by opening with a proposal that's easy to comply with.

4. Early on in the exchanges, ask a question to which you already know the answer. If the other party corroborates, good. If not, you've learned something very valuable: Your opposite number is either misinformed on that point or is not leveling with you. You will need to proceed with some care.

5. Ask for more than you realistically can expect to get. This common negotiating tool leaves you room for maneuvering, for advancing alternatives or counter-proposals, and for establishing a fallback position.

6. As the bargaining proceeds, make it a give-and-take session. Give the other party some small victories, putting up only a token fight on minor points. Have a list of items that are vital to you, as well as a second list of items of little concern. For example, if you're negotiating to buy a house, your primary objectives are getting the house you want, at an overall cost within your means, and at monthly payments you can afford. These three factors constitute your "important" list, plus perhaps a new roof or new plumbing (which you've deemed important because of their cost). You may not, however, be concerned about the length of escrow (the process during which documents are compiled and the buyer's money is transferred to the seller), and are willing to compromise on this item. You may also be willing to make your own arrangements for certain minor, but necessary, repairs.

In other words, leave the other person some room for maneuvering. An inflexible stance weakens the opportunity for compromise; and compromise is essential to all successful negotiation.

7. Keep psychological motivations in mind. Occasionally they can be more important than monetary ones. When someone sells his own house, for example, he may care more about selling to a

sound, reputable family than he does about attaining top dollar. My friend Richard Whittey, a small business specialist, recently told me a story about two partners who were selling their business for "personal reasons." Richard was interested in buying the business and sensed the tension between the current owners, who had apparently been unable to patch up long-standing differences about how the business should be run.

After several hours of negotiating on three different occasions, Richard quietly offered $1 million in cash to the owners, who had asked for $5 million over a three-year period. Needless to say, everyone in the room — attorneys for both sides as well as the partners — was shocked. Two days later, the partners accepted the deal with only minor changes.

I asked Richard what prompted him to make such a relatively low offer. His answer was interesting. Aside from the fact that he felt the asking price was exhorbitant, he knew the cash offer would allow the partners to get out quickly and go their separate ways. In order to end the feuding that had plagued them for months, they decided it was worthwhile to accept the cash right away and sever their partnership without further delay, *in spite of the fact that it amounted to much less than the longer-term arrangements.* In this case, purely emotional motivations had played an important role in settling the agreement satisfactorily for all parties involved.

8. Always try to have an associate present during negotiations if you possibly can, particularly if his or her presence is relevant to your business and/or the negotiations themselves. (Obviously, some negotiations are conducted by phone, and some are best conducted alone.) If your partner cannot make the meeting for any reason, postpone it. You may think you're the equal of any number of opponents, but it's not that simple. Two heads are often better than one, and unless you have a fabulously retentive memory, you won't recall everything that was said, and how it was said. Having at least one associate with you can double the persuasive power you can muster. Find out beforehand who your

adversaries are and how many there will be. If they have five on their side, you should bring at least three to yours.

Another advantage to having at least one ally is that it enables you to observe the "body language" of the opposition. While you're talking and arguing, your confederate can be watching. Physical signs and movements—the crossing of arms, a jiggling foot and scores of other twitches and gestures—can tell an experienced observer what the other person is thinking.

9. Be prepared, and willing, to listen after presenting your viewpoints. Have a list of questions that you need answered, and then listen *carefully* to the other person's point of view. this can be the key to closing a deal successfully and amicably.

10. Make sure that you clearly understand—and make the most of—*all* of your options. If you're trying to buy a house and the seller turns down your offer because he or she is firm on the price, leave the door open by concluding your meeting on a pleasant note. "Thanks for your time. We really like the house, but $98,500 is our limit; should your situation change, please call us." Not only is it a cordial exit line, it gives the other party plenty of room to reopen with a counter-offer.

Then take the time to analyze the true source of your negotiation problems. Were you worried about making the monthly payment, or coming up with the down payment? Or were you simply placing too much emphasis on the overall amount? Always keep in mind that there are plenty of other houses available, and there's bound to be another one out there that's just right for you. This will help you avoid the trap of *forcing* yourself to make a deal, especially if it's not advantageous for you.

11. When basic agreement has been established, put it in writing, even if it's not the ultimate, refined version. Getting something in writing effects an immediate commitment. Don't necessarily wait for fancy typing. Handwriting is perfectly valid, and both parties should sign then and there. In many negotiations this principle will apply. People, being human, change their

minds; many an agreement has broken down while the parties waited for neatly typed copies in quintuplicate. Take it upon yourself to pin the deal down — in writing — when *you're* ready.

12. After an agreement has been reached, stop the meeting, stop selling, and stop talking. You already have what you want. Don't risk fouling things up. As salespeople have learned to their dismay, many a sale has been lost after it's been made simply because both parties continued talking. So when the papers have been signed, don't feel like you have to make the other person a lifelong friend or offer an invitation to lunch or cocktails.

Confronting Your Fears

In the course of negotiating, some people find that their biggest roadblock is their own personal fear of the process itself, which can easily overshadow the true issues of the deal.

Clearly identifying your fears before entering any negotiation can make the difference between directing your energies effectively toward completing a deal, and unwittingly expending them in breaking up the deal. If you feel confused and uncertain without understanding why, chances are you'll hold back and disagree with the other party at every turn in the negotiation. You may know, fundamentally, what it is that you want, but emotional and irrational factors, however invisible, could prevent you from reaching your true goals.

Confront your fears first and assess their validity, and then equip yourself to counter them with strong, positive action. Do some research, if necessary; sometimes getting at the facts helps immensely in easing your fears. The old adage, "99 percent of what you worry about never comes to pass," could be an appropriate reminder at this point. Don't let your fears control you; consider them with your own *rational* arguments.

Let's take a relatively simple example. You're buying a house. The asking price is $98,000 and the best you can do is $90,000. Get out your pencil and pad and set up two columns. Label the left-hand side "What I Want," the other side "What They Want." Filling in this list will define your negotiation perimeters. At the top of each column, write down the price—theirs and yours. Then move down the left-hand side. You want them to pay title insurance and any and all necessary repairs prior to the sale. Next, look at their side and try to analyze what they want.

Now you can evaluate what you may have to give up for that $8,000 spread. You or someone you know may be a talented carpenter or electrician, in which case you may be able to arrange for the repairs yourself. You may want to pick up the escrow costs (they probably will amount to only $500); perhaps the title insurance costs as well. A careful, itemized breakdown of these costs (part of doing your homework) will enable you to enter into the negotiations with confidence.

Don't give them your cost total, ever. Just reel off in your own good time what you are prepared to do. There are many, many variables in a real estate deal. You may find that they're interested in a quick escrow (30 days or sooner) or a slow escrow (three to six months). You will want to take that into consideration. If they want a 30-day escrow, which is extremely short, you may want to tell them that in exchange for the $8,000 you will be able to move that quickly. Pay particular attention to their response to your query: "How fast do you want to move?" How desperate are they? Does it appear as though there are other buyers in the picture? These, of course, are all extremely important points.

Rehearsing for Negotiation

Rehearsal for the drama of negotiation is also highly advisable. Bargaining is the country cousin of the theatrical arts. You should work up a scenario well in advance, a game plan embracing introductory gambits, diversionary suggestions, counter-proposals, crucial arguments, and final position. If you don't, you'll be like an actor who hasn't learned her lines — and you'll feel every bit as foolish. Role-playing is a big help. Days before you enter into negotiation you may undergo intellectual and emotional conditioning by having an associate play the part of your adversary in as hard-headed a manner as you can expect from your opposite numbers at the bargaining table. This can "psych you up" for the sessions. And it is fun to be psychologically honed for the forthcoming big match.

When I say that negotiating is a form of theatre, I mean that a certain amount of thespian ability is extremely helpful. So is a poker face. Pretended disinterest in an adversary's proposal, while you cite possible alternatives to those suggestions, is likely provide you with an advantage: It will put him on the defensive, in the position of selling you — even if secretly you are quite willing to be sold on his proposition.

You'll find that one of the most effective bargaining weapons is silence. Nothing unnerves an adversary so much as an impassive, inscrutable, unresponsive exterior. I'm not suggesting, however, that you play *Shogun* or behave rudely. Just realize that you don't have to respond to every comment; listening carefully can help you to assess your adversary's motives and tactics.

You may, while negotiating, find the temptation to fill the silences almost irresistible. Resist, nonetheless. A highly successful real estate broker told me she lost out on a sale of a very big piece of industrial property early in her career because, in the face of her adversaries' stolid silence and her own nervousness, she gave away too much.

A display of controlled anger can also be effective if it is used in a very special circumstance with people who might be impressed by it. But don't overdo it. If you start raging, you may find yourself with no alternative but to stalk out of the bargaining session.

There are several vital don'ts connected with the art of

negotiation.

1. If possible, never go into a negotiation unless you're in top shape, physically and mentally; never negotiate when you're upset, sad, tired or sick. Remember: The deal you negotiate today, whether it involves real estate, a raise, a new car, or a million-dollar contract, you will have to live with from that point onward. To be sure you go into the match in top form, at the peak of your capabilities, and able to tell yourself that you've done the very best job you could.

2. Don't assume the other party has the same motivations you do. Everyone comes to a negotiation with a different set of objectives and needs. Your job is to define as quickly as possible your needs and the other side's needs.

3. Don't drag a lawyer along until you need one. Lawyers cost lots of money. Recently, in preparation for a meeting, I had a brief conference with an attorney to go over what I should do in case the deal should seem ready to wrap up. I spent a short, solid thirty minutes with her, took extensive notes on her advice, and felt armed with enough to get through the meeting. (And I made sure I knew where and how to get in touch with her if I needed her during the negotiations.)

The presence of legal eagles tends to scare everybody. If you bring a lawyer, the other side will quite naturally want to bring one, too. This can often eliminate any of the necessary, casual give-and-take. People are prone to become unduly formal, even inflexible, in the company of lawyers. As an associate once put it: "Lawyers are often more interested in making things legal than in making the deal." Which is as it should be — things should be legal. But there's a time and place for everything, and in the early stages of negotiation the bargaining should take priority.

4. If you have an associate with you during a bargaining session, don't be afraid to suggest a break in the meeting to discuss strategy. It's perfectly all right to say that you want to discuss with your partner a few points outside the conference room. Simply

excuse yourself, take a walk in the hallway, or go out for a cup of coffee. This "time-out" is a good way to digest the latest events and decide on the best appropriate action.

There is great leverage in this tactic, if used wisely. Such a maneuver can bemuse the opposition. But you should never use it if by doing so you appear indecisive or confused. Then you will lose far more than you can hope to gain.

5. Don't agree on any given point — or to the entire package — too quickly. "Bargains made in speed are commonly repented at leisure" — a wise rule of thumb. Don't let yourself be hurried unduly; think the deal through with slow and measured care. Twenty-four hours, if you need it, is a reasonable amount of reflection time.

6. Once you've given your word, stick to it. There is nothing that will destroy your standing more soundly than a reputation for reneging on a deal. If a deal is wrong for you, the time to say so is *before* you formally agree to it.

7. Don't be afraid to walk out, if a crucial point is at issue, or if tempers are getting frayed. (It's preferable to getting into a shouting match.) If the other side doesn't call you back, you can always return anyway. And if you are called back, that's usually a sign that the opposition is weakening.

8. Finally, never, never assume that the other party isn't as intelligent or able as you are. More disasters arise from underestimating the capacities of one's opponent than from any other single mistake. The shock engendered from a miscalculation of this sort will place you at a disadvantage from which you won't easily recover.

Whether you're buying or selling, you should always be the salesman in negotiating. Even if you're buying, you have to sell the seller on the idea that he's doing the right thing. This is particularly important if you're buying, for instance, a family business, in which case the idea of continuity is important. You have to persuade the seller that you're worthy of maintaining his family's business.

A Note from the Author

What I most wanted to do in this book was to shatter the mystique that has kept women from enjoying the confidence—and the fun—that comes with making money. Because making money *is* fun, as I hope I have shown in these pages. But it is much more than that, too. It is the key to your security, your independence, and your success as a mature human being. Creatively pursued, the money game is the most exciting game of all! Join those of us who've found that financial awareness has brought immense satisfaction and a rewarding life-style. We did it, and so can you . . . now go to it!

Paula Nelson
Santa Monica, California
September 1986

About the Author

Paula Nelson is known to millions as a financial commentator on NBC's "Today Show." She is a frequent guest expert on "Hour Magazine," "Merv Griffin" and other national news shows. Her byline has appeared in *Newsweek, Saturday Evening Post* and many major American newspapers. She lectures frequently to Fortune 500 companies, financial institutions and small business groups and associations. She now serves on the board of directors of two California corporations, and heads The Money Forum, a company devoted to financial education.